Wei-Chuan Cooking School was founded in 1961 as a subsidiary of Wei-Chuan Food Corporation, the largest food manufacturer in Taiwan. The school soon became the largest and most respected institution of its kind along the Asia-Pacific rim. Graduates include world-class chefs, institutional teachers, professional caterers, connoisseurs of Chinese and international cuisines as well as many homemakers.

As Wei-Chuan's reputation grew, requests came from all over the world for guidance and information relative to the recipes used in the cooking classes. In an effort to meet this demand, **CHINESE CUISINE** was written and published in 1972. The book was very successful and became the first in a series of Wei-Chuan Cookbooks. Wei-Chuan Publishing was founded later that same year in Taipei with a branch subsequently established in the U.S.A. in 1978.

Wei-Chuan, long recognized as publishing the most comprehensive Chinese cuisine cookbooks, has now expanded its recipes to include other cuisines from around the world.

Wei-Chuan's success can be attributed to its commitment to provide the best quality product possible. All recipes are complemented by full color photographs. Each recipe is written simply with easy-to-follow instructions and precisely measured ingredients. Wei-Chuan stands behind its name, reputation, and commitment to remain true to the authenticity of its recipes.

La Escuela de Cocina Wei-Chuan fue fundada en 1961 como subsidiaria de Wei-Chuan Food Corporation, fabricante de comida más grande en Taiwán. La escuela pronto se convirtió en la institución más grande y respetada de su clase en el aro del Pacífico-Asiático. Nuestros graduados incluyen chefs reconocidos mundialmente, profesores institucionales, abastecedores profesionales y conocedores de cocina china y cocinas internacionales como también amas de casa.

Mientras la reputación de Wei-Chuan creció, se recibían solicitudes de todas partes del mundo pidiendo consejos e información pertinentes a las recetas usadas en las clases de cocina. En un esfuerzo para satisfacer este requerimiento, *CHINESE CUISINE* fue escrito y publicado en 1972. El libro fue un gran éxito y el primero en una serie de Libros de Cocina de Wei-Chuan. La casa editorial Wei-Chuan fue fundada, luego ese mismo año en Taipeh, seguida por una sucursal establecida en E.U. en 1978.

La compañía Wei-Chuan reconocida por largo tiempo como la editora de los libros más completos de comida china, ha expandido sus recetas que ahora incluyen otras cocinas de diferentes partes del mundo.

El éxito de Wei-Chuan se debe a su compromiso en proveer el producto de más alta calidad posible. Casi todas las recetas se complementan con fotografías a todo color. Cada receta está escrita con instrucciones fáciles de seguir y con ingredientes meticulosamente medidos. Wei-Chuan respalda su nombre, su reputación y su compromiso en mantenerse fiel a la autenticidad de sus recetas.

We would like to give our special note of thanks to the following retailers who helped in many ways to make this book look the way it does.

Quadrille
Kottoya, Inc.
McMullen's Japanese Antiques
Mutual Trading Co., Inc.
Lalique

Editor
Huang Su-Huei
Authors
Jia-Tzu Yeh (Chinese cuisine)
Diane Soliz-Martese (Mexican & Italian)
Victor Chang (Japanese cuisine)
Sukhum Kittivech (Thai cuisine)

English Translation
Innie Hua
Meghan Chen
Chinese Translation
Sophia Lin
Chang-Yen C. Shen
Spanish Translation
Paul Andersen
Sylvia Jiménez-Andersen
María Teresa Aguirre
Editorial Staff
Sophia Lin
Yen-Jen Lai
John Holt
Elsa Lee

Art Direction
F.S. Chang
Photography
Irene Chang
Design
AGP Productions, Inc.
Yvette Mah
Production Assistance
Vincent Wong

PRINTED IN TAIWAN, R.O.C.
China Color Printing Co., Ltd.

WEI-CHUAN PUBLISHING
1455 Monterey Pass Road, #110
Monterey Park, CA 91754, U. S. A.
Tel: 213-261-3880
Fax: 213-261-3299

FIRST PRINTING, OCTOBER 1995
ISBN 0-941676-56-0
(English/Chinese/Spanish)

編輯
黃淑惠
作者
葉佳祖（中國菜）
絲黛安（墨西哥，義大利菜）
張勝利（日本菜）
齊舒肯（泰國菜）

英文翻譯
華茵
陳美君
中文翻譯
林淑華
陳常彥
西文翻譯
安保羅
安西雅
馬利亞
文稿協助
林淑華
賴燕貞
何久恩
李愛茜

設計編輯
張方馨
攝影
章靄琳
設計
AGP Produtions Inc.
馬紀雯
英西文排版
黃穎新
中文排版
甘露資訊印刷有限公司

印刷
中華彩色印刷股份有限公司

味全出版社有限公司
台北市仁愛路四段28號2樓
郵政劃撥00182038號　味全出版社帳戶
電話：(02)702-1148・702-1149
傳真：(02)704-2729

版權所有：局版台業字第0179號
中華民國84年10月初版
定價：新台幣貳佰捌拾元整

Editor
Huang Su-Huei
Autores
Jia-Tzu Yeh (Chinese cuisine)
Diane Soliz-Martese (Mexican & Italian)
Victor Chang (Japanese cuisine)
Sukhum Kittivech (Thai cuisine)

Traducción al Inglés
Innie Hua
Meghan Chen
Traducción al Chino
Sophia Lin
Chang-Yen C. Shen
Traducción al Español
Paul Andersen
Sylvia Jiménez-Andersen
María Teresa Aguírre
Asistentes del Editor
Shophia Lin
Yen-Jen Lai
John Holt
Elsa Lee

Dirección Artística
F.S. Chang
Fotografía
Irene Chang
Diseño del Libro
AGP Productions, Inc.
Yvette Mah
Pre-Impresión
Vincent Wong

Impreso en Taiwán, R.O.C.

Derechos
Wei-Chuan Publishing
1455 Monterey Pass Road, #110
Monterey Park, CA 91754, U.S.A.
Tel: 213-261-3880
Fax: 213-261-3299

One Dish Meals

COCINA POPULAR DE UN SOLO PLATILLO

簡餐

五國風味

Table of Contents 目錄 Contenido

Conversion Table　　量器介紹　　Tabla de Conversión

1 cup (1 c.) = 236 c.c.

1 杯(1 飯碗)=16 大匙　　taza (tz.)

1 tablespoon (1 T.) = 15 c.c.

1 大匙(1 湯匙)　　cucharada (C.)

1 teaspoon (1 t.) = 5 c.c.

1 小匙(1 茶匙)　　cucharadita (c.)

About the Authors

Jia-Tzu Yeh has been enchanted by the fine art of Chinese cooking since childhood. At age 18, he apprenticed with famed Master Chef Peng Chang Kuei, a leading expert in Hunan cuisine. After three years of rigorous training, Mr. Yeh became chef Peng's most accomplished apprentice.

Mr. Yeh's 30-year experience and talents are manifested in Hunan cooking and dim sum. Superb Chinese cooking must embody three important qualities: color, aroma, and taste. Mr. Yeh's creations boast all three, earning him tremendous critical and consumer acclaim in Taiwan as well as the U. S. Mr. Yeh has repeatedly been invited to assume the Master Chef post in various dining establishments in Japan and in the U. S.

Beyond Mr. Yeh's achievements as a culinary artist, he has devoted much of his work and attention to writing cookbooks to promote the art of Chinese cuisine. Wei Chuan's publication *Chinese Cooking For Beginners* benefited from Mr. Yeh's generous guidance and advice.

Diane Soliz-Martese is the author of the very successful cookbook *Mexican Cooking Made Easy*. This outstanding book is sold internationally and is carried in the libraries of many cities in the U. S.

Diane acquired cooking skills as a natural part of her Italian and Mexican heritage. She had the unique opportunity to learn the traditional meals of both countries in a very special way. Her father, John Martese was the owner and Master Chef of the well known and popular El Zorro restaurant in Lake Tahoe, California.

Diane has learned and perfected the culinary skills passed on to her from both cultures. Many of her recipes are from her father's collection as well as special recipes from her extended Italian and Mexican families. Diane has perfected these recipes in such a way that they can be easily followed and prepared with ingredients commonly available.

作者介紹

葉佳祖先生自幼即對中國食藝十分嚮往，18歲拜師於湖南菜名廚彭長貴先生的門下，習藝三年出師，爲彭氏的得意門生。

葉先生積三十餘年的經驗，對湖南菜及中式點心尤爲獨到，其做工別緻精細，色、香、味俱全，甚得中外人士的喜愛，前總統夫人蔣宋美齡女士亦對其餐點讚譽有加。

自民國56年以來葉先生即多次受邀至日本及美國掌理廚藝。日本知名的婦女雜誌「主婦之友」亦曾於其烹飪專欄介紹葉先生的「中國料理」。

葉先生不但廚藝佳更積極參與著作食譜的工作，希望將中國烹飪的藝術廣爲推介。本公司所出版的「中國菜實用專輯」即曾得葉先生的大力協助。

絲黛安女士是味全暢銷食譜「墨西哥菜」的作者，這本食譜行銷多國、並爲美國許多圖書館所收存。

黛安女士的一手好廚藝受惠於其家庭良多，她的墨裔母親和義裔烹飪好手的父親都對她在追求食的藝術上有極大的影響，其父曾在北加州的名勝地「太浩湖」開了一家頗負盛名的「El Zorro」墨西哥餐館，並親自擔任主廚。

在這本新書中，黛安還收錄了許多她父親及親友珍藏的義大利及墨西哥菜的食譜，她以精進的廚藝和豐富的經驗將這些食譜重新製作改良，用簡單易學的方法寫出，並採用日常中容易取得的材料來製作，務求簡易實用，人人都可做，享受家中烹飪的樂趣。

Sobre los Autores

Jia-Tzu Yeh ha estado fascinado por el arte de la cocina china desde su niñez. A los 18 años fue aprendiz del famoso Maestro, Chef Peng Chang Huei, principal experto en cocina Hunan. Después de tres años de rigurosa práctica el Sr. Yeh llegó a ser el mejor aprendiz del Chef Peng.

Los 30 años de experiencia y talentos del Sr. Yeh se manifiestan en la cocina Hunan y dim sum. La exquisita cocina china debe incorporar tres importantes cualidades: color, aroma, y sabor. Las creaciones del Sr. Yeh exaltan las tres, haciéndolo merecedor de la ovación de los críticos y de los consumidores tanto en Taiwan como en E.E.U.U. El Sr. Yeh ha sido invitado frecuentemente para asumir el puesto de Maestro Chef en diversos establecimientos en Japón y E.E.U.U.

Además del éxito del Sr. Yeh como artista culinario, él ha dedicado gran parte de su trabajo y atención a escribir libros para promover el arte de la cocina china. La publicación de *Cocina China Para Principiantes* de Wei-Chuan se benefició con la generosa guía y consejo del Sr. Yeh.

Diane Soliz-Martese es la autora del exitoso libro *Comida Mexicana Fácil de Preparar*. Este magnífico libro se vende internacionalmente y se encuentra en las bibliotecas de muchas ciudades estadounidenses.

Diane adquirió sus habilidades culinarias como algo natural de sus dos herencias, la italiana y la mexicana. Tuvo la singular oportunidad de aprender los platillos tradicionales de ambos países en una forma muy especial. Su padre, John Martese, fue el dueño y Chef Principal del popular y renombrado restaurante El Zorro en Lake Tahoe, California.

Diane aprendió y perfeccionó las habilidades que le fueron pasadas de sus dos culturas. Muchas de las recetas provienen de la colección de su padre y también de sus familias, italiana y mexicana. Diane ha perfeccionado estas recetas de tal manera que se pueden seguir fácilmente y preparar con ingredientes fáciles de obtener.

Victor Chang is both the owner and chief chef of the Yamaha Japanese Restaurant in Pasadena, California.

Prior to becoming proficient in the art of Japanese cooking, Mr. Chang delved into the regional specialties of Chinese cuisine in the northern and Szechwan Provinces. After many years of perfecting his craft in Northern Region Chinese cuisine, his culinary senses were piqued by the unique sweet and sour blending of Japanese cuisine. He soon followed in the steps of the great chefs of Japan and mastered this new art form which so intrigued him.

For many years chef Chang has been developing and perfecting his craft in Japanese cuisine aiming to better his best creations. A decade after establishing his Yamaha Japanese Restaurant, now a well-loved member of the Pasadena dining community, he enjoys the loyalty of his many patrons and new diners.

張勝利先生是南加州帕沙迪那市著名的日本料理店〝山葉日式餐廳〞的業主並兼掌主廚。

張先生在涉歷日式料理前曾浸淫中國北方菜及川菜多年，後因對日本和食藝術發生興趣，從而拜日本名師習藝。

多年來張先生在〝日式料理〞及〝壽司〞上潛心研究，精益求精。創店十多年亦曾多次蒙洛杉磯時報、帕市周報等媒體的推介報導，極受當地人士的歡迎。

Victor Chang es el dueño y el Chef Principal del Yamaha Japanese Resturant en Pasadena, California.

Antes de llegar a ser un experto en el arte de la cocina japonesa, el Sr. Chang exploró las especialidades de la cocina china en las provincias del norte y Szechwan. Después de pasar muchos años perfeccionando su práctica en la cocina de la Región del Norte de China, sus sentidos culinarios se estimularon por la singular mezcla agridulce de la cocina japonesa. Inmediatamente siguió los pasos de los grandes chefs de Japón y perfeccionó esta nueva forma artística que tanto le fascinaba.

Por muchos años el Chef Chang ha estado desarrollando y perfeccionando su arte de la cocina japonesa con el propósito de mejorar sus excelentes creaciones. Una década después de establecer su restaurante japonés Yamaha, ahora un miembro tan querido de la comunidad culinaria de Pasadena, él disfruta de la lealtad tanto de sus muchos patrocinadores como de sus nuevos clientes

---

Sukhum (Ken) Kittivech brought his extensive knowledge of authentic Thai cooking to the U.S.A. and opened his first Chan Dara restaurant in Southern California in the early 1970's. The excellent reputation of his dishes grew rapidly and it was only a short time before two additional restaurants were opened.

In 1992, Sukhum put his knowledge and dedication to perfection by authoring the very popular *Thai Cooking Made Easy*, currently in its second printing.

Chef Kittivech is one of those special people who can continually create new dishes of the most delicious mouth-watering flavors. In this newest cookbook, he has carefully designed his one-dish-meal recipes so that each exotic and tasty dish can be easily and successfully prepared at home.

齊舒肯先生於1970年代初期在南加州開設了他的第一家泰式餐廳〝Chan Dara〞，將他對傳統泰國菜的豐富經歷帶入美國市場。由此他道地出色的泰國菜即廣受歡迎，且聲譽日隆，目前在南加州已擁有三家泰式餐廳。

1992年齊先生受本公司之邀著作〝味全泰國菜〞食譜，更將其精湛的廚藝付諸文字。此本食譜十分暢銷，1995年已印至第三版。

齊先生是一位極有創意的廚師，他的菜式常有新意，在這本新簡餐食譜中他精選了多樣的菜色都是十分可口別緻，並經專業廚師、職業婦女及家庭主婦試做後，一致公認製作簡易風味特佳，是一本不可多得的好食譜。

Sukhum (Ken) Kittivech trajo su extenso conocimiento de la auténtica cocina Thai a E.E.U.U. y abrió su primer restaurante Chan Dara en el sur de California a principios de 1970. La excelente reputación de sus platillos creció rápidamente y en muy poco tiempo abrió dos nuevos restaurantes.

En 1992, Sukhum aplicó su conocimiento y dedicación a la perfección siendo el autor del muy popular *Thai Cooking Made Easy*, ahora en su segunda impresión.

Chef Kittivech es una de esas personas especiales que constantemente crean nuevos platillos de los sabores más exquisitos. En este nuevo libro de cocina, ha diseñado cuidadosamente sus propias recetas de un solo platillo para que cada exótico y sabroso platillo se pueda preparar fácil y exitosamente en casa.

Chicken & Chestnuts Over Rice
Pollo y Castañas Sobre Arroz

栗子燒鷄飯

1

2

3

- Serves 2 -

$^2/_3$ lb. (300g) boneless Chicken
or Pork, cut in pieces
(Fig. 1)

10 Fresh chestnuts (shelled,
Fig. 2) or canned
chestnuts or potato
(cut in pieces)

1 5 cloves of garlic, sliced
$^1/_2$ star anise
6 ginger slices
6 green onion sections (white
part), 2" (5 cm) long

2 3 T. rice wine (Fig. 3) or
cooking wine
1 T. rock candy
2 $^1/_2$ T. soy sauce
$^1/_2$ T. dark soy sauce
(See p. 12, Fig. 2)

6 green onion sections (green
part), 2" (5 cm) long

2 c. cooked rice

1 Heat 4 T. oil. Stir-fry **1** until garlic turns brown. Add chicken and chestnuts; fry 4 minutes (remove some oil if desired). Add **2** and cook 7 minutes over medium heat until sauce is partially evaporated; stir during cooking. Sprinkle in green onions and stir-fry briefly.

2 Put rice on 2 serving plates, and top with the chicken and chestnuts. Serve with vegetables.

■ 1 1/3 lb. (600g) pork ribs may be used for 2/3 lb. (300g) boneless chicken. Add one more cup of water after adding the ribs to **2** ; bring to boil. Reduce heat to medium and cook 25 minutes. Other procedures are the same as above.

- 2人份 -

鷄或豬腿肉（切塊，圖1）
‥‥‥‥‥半斤（300公克）

鮮栗（去皮，圖2）或罐頭栗
子或馬鈴薯（切塊）‥‥10個

1 蒜（切片）‥‥‥‥‥‥5瓣
八角 ‥‥‥‥‥‥‥‥$^1/_2$朶
薑 ‥‥‥‥‥‥‥‥‥6片
蔥白（切5公分長）‥‥‥6支

2 紹興酒或米酒（圖3）‥‥3大匙
冰糖 ‥‥‥‥‥‥‥1大匙
醬油 ‥‥‥‥‥‥2 $^1/_2$大匙
老抽（深色醬油見12頁，圖2）
‥‥‥‥‥‥‥‥‥$^1/_2$大匙

蔥綠（5公分長）‥‥‥‥6段

飯 ‥‥‥‥‥‥‥‥‥2碗

1 油4大匙燒熱，放入 **1** 料炒至蒜呈金黃色，隨入鷄肉及栗子煎炸約4分鐘（若油太多，可倒出部份），再加 **2** 料不蓋鍋改中火煮約7分鐘，中途翻拌至汁略收乾，撒上蔥綠略炒即成。

2 盤內盛飯，上置栗子燒鷄與蔬菜配食。

■ 若用豬排骨1斤取代鷄腿肉半斤，放入 **2** 料後再加水1杯燒開，改中火煮25分鐘，其他作法與上面同。

- 2 porciones -

$^2/_3$ lb. (300g) pollo o cerdo
sin hueso, cortado en
pedazos (Fig. 1)

10 castañas frescas (sin
cáscara, Fig. 2) o castañas
enlatadas o papa (cortada
en pedazos)

1 5 dientes de ajo, picado
$^1/_2$ anís estrella
6 rebanadas de jengibre
6 pedazos de cebollín (parte
blanca), 2" (5 cm) de
largo

2 3 C. vino de arroz (Fig. 3)
o vino para cocinar
1 C. azúcar cristal
2 $^1/_2$ C. salsa de soya
$^1/_2$ C. salsa de soya oscura
(vea p. 12, Fig. 2)

6 pedazos de cebollín (parte
verde), 2" (5 cm) de largo

2 tz. arroz cocido

1 Caliente 4 C. de aceite. Fría-revolviendo **1** hasta que se dore el ajo. Agregue el pollo y las castañas; fría por 4 minutos (quítele aceite si lo desea). Agregue **2** y cocine por 7 minutos a fuego moderado hasta que la salsa esté medio evaporada; revuelva mientras se cocina. Espolvoréele los cebollines y fría-revolviendo brevemente.

2 Divida el arroz en los 2 platos a servir, y cubra con el pollo y las castañas. Sirva con vegetales.

■ Puede usar 1 1/3 lbs. (600g) costillas de cerdo por 2/3 lb. (300g) de pollo sin hueso. Agregue una taza más de agua después de agregar las costillas a **2** ; haga hervir. Baje el fuego a moderado y cocine por 25 minutos. Las otras instrucciones son como lo indicado en la receta.

Hunan Tofu
Tofu Hunan

湖南豆腐

- Serves 2 -

3 pieces tofu, $^3/_4$ lb. (340g)

$^1/_3$ lb. (150g) lean meat (pork, beef or chicken)

1 | 1 t. each: soy sauce, cooking wine, cornstarch

2 | 1 T. fermented black beans
3 green onions, cut 2" (5 cm) long

3 | 2 $^1/_2$ T. soy sauce
1 t. dark soy sauce (See p. 12, Fig. 2)
1 t. hot sauce paste
$^1/_2$ T. sesame oil
1 T. cooking wine
1 c. stock
1 T. cornstarch

2 c. cooked rice

1. Cut tofu in pieces (Fig. 1). Slice meat (Fig. 2), then mix well with **1** . Rinse black beans.

2. Heat 2 T. oil. Stir-fry meat until separated and cooked; remove the meat.

3. Stir-fry **2** (Fig. 3) with the remaining oil until fragrant. Add mixture **3** and tofu; bring to boil. Cook uncovered, over high heat 5 minutes (stir during cooking). Add cooked meat and mix well. Pour on top of rice and serve with vegetables.

– 2人份 –

豆腐　3大塊（9兩，340公克）

瘦肉（豬、牛或鷄）
　　　………4兩（150公克）

1 | 醬油　…………………1小匙
酒　……………………1小匙
玉米粉　………………1小匙

2 | 豆豉　…………………1大匙
蔥（切5公分長）………3支

3 | 醬油　………………2 $^1/_2$大匙
老抽（深色醬油見12頁，圖2）
　　…………………1小匙
辣椒醬　………………1小匙
麻油　………………$^1/_2$大匙
酒　……………………1大匙
高湯　…………………1杯
玉米粉　………………1大匙

飯　……………………2碗

1. 豆腐切塊（圖1），瘦肉切片（圖2）調 **1** 料拌勻，豆豉略洗。

2. 油2大匙燒熱，將肉炒開至熟撈出。

3. 餘油炒香 **2** 料（圖3），隨入調勻的 **3** 料及豆腐燒開，不蓋鍋以大火燒煮5分鐘（中途需翻拌），再入炒好的肉拌勻，置飯上與蔬菜配食。

- 2 porciones -

3 pedazos de tofu, $^3/_4$ lb. (340g)

$^1/_3$ lb. (150g) carne magra (cerdo, res o pollo)

1 | 1 c. c/u: salsa de soya, vino para cocinar, maicena

2 | 1 C. frijoles negros fermentados
3 cebollines, cortados en 2" (5 cm) de largo

3 | 2 $^1/_2$ C. salsa de soya
1 c. salsa de soya oscura (vea p. 12, Fig. 2)
1 c. pasta de salsa picante
$^1/_2$ C. aceite de sésamo
1 C. vino para cocinar
1 tz. caldo
1 C. maicena

2 tz. arroz cocido

1. Corte el tofu en pedazos (Fig. 1). Rebane la carne (Fig. 2), luego mezcle bien con **1** . Enjuague los frijoles.

2. Caliente 2 C. de aceite. Fría-revolviendo la carne hasta que se separe y se cocine; retire la carne.

3. Fría-revolviendo **2** (Fig. 3) con el aceite restante hasta que esté aromático. Agregue la mezcla **3** y el tofu; haga hervir. Cocine sin tapar a fuego alto por 5 minutos (revuelva mientras se cocina). Agregue la carne cocida y mezcle bien. Vacíe sobre el arroz y sirva con vegetales.

Sweet & Sour Pork Over Rice
Cerdo Agridulce Sobre Arroz

糖醋肉飯

1

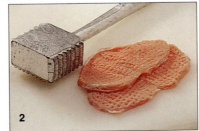

2

3

- Serves 2 -

¹/₂ lb. (225g) lean meat (pork, beef or chicken)

1 | ²/₃ T. soy sauce
1 egg (small, beaten)

6 T. cornstarch

3 c. oil for deep-frying

2 | Total of ¹/₂ lb. (225g), cut in pieces (Fig. 1): onion, green bell pepper, carrot & tomato

1 T. minced garlic

3 | ²/₃ t. salt
3 T. each: sugar, vinegar, ketchup
1 ¹/₂ T. cornstarch
6 T. water

2 c. cooked rice

---

1. Slice meat ²/₃" (1.5 cm) thick; tenderize with meat mallet (Fig. 2). Then cut in 1" (2.5 cm) pieces; mix well with **1** . Put the meat pieces and cornstarch in a plastic bag; shake the bag to coat the meat evenly (Fig. 3).

2. Heat oil for deep-frying. Add in meat pieces one by one (Deep-fry in two batches if oil is not enough to cover the meat); deep-fry meat pieces over high heat 2 minutes until crispy and cooked. Remove.

3. Heat 1 T. oil. Add **2** and 1 T. water; stir-fry briefly then remove. Wipe wok clean; heat 2 T. oil. Stir-fry minced garlic until fragrant; add mixture **3** and bring to boil. Add meat pieces and **2** ; stir-fry until mixed well. Remove; place on top of rice and serve with vegetables.

■ Meat pieces may be deep-fried then frozen in advance. Bake 10 minutes in preheated oven at 450°F (230°C) when ready to use.

- 2人份 -

瘦肉（豬、牛或鷄）
‥‥‥‥‥6兩（225公克）

1 | 醬油 ‥‥‥‥‥‥²/₃大匙
蛋（小的，打散）‥‥‥1個

玉米粉 ‥‥‥‥‥‥6大匙

「炸油」‥‥‥‥‥‥3杯

2 | 洋蔥、青椒、紅蘿蔔、番茄
切塊（圖1）共6兩（225公克）

蒜末 ‥‥‥‥‥‥1大匙

3 | 鹽 ‥‥‥‥‥‥²/₃小匙
糖、醋、番茄醬 ‥‥各3大匙
玉米粉 ‥‥‥‥‥1 ¹/₂大匙
水 ‥‥‥‥‥‥6大匙

飯 ‥‥‥‥‥‥2碗

---

1. 肉切1.5公分厚片、搥鬆（圖2），再切2.5公分塊狀，調 **1** 料拌勻；與玉米粉裝入袋內翻滾，使均勻裹上粉（圖3）。

2. 「炸油」燒熱，將肉一塊塊全部放入（若炸油減半，可分二次炸）大火炸約2分鐘至表面酥脆肉熟撈出。

3. 油1大匙燒熱，將 **2** 料加水1大匙略炒熱鏟出，擦乾鍋面；加油2大匙燒熱，炒香蒜末，隨入調勻的 **3** 料攪拌燒開，再加肉塊及 **2** 料炒拌均勻，置飯上與生菜配食。

■ 肉可先炸好冷凍，使用時將烤箱燒熱，以450℉（230℃）烤10分鐘至熱加入煮好的糖醋汁（**3** 料）即可。

- 2 porciones -

¹/₂ lb. (225g) carne magra (cerdo, res o pollo)

1 | ²/₃ C. salsa de soya
1 huevo (chico, batido)

6 C. maicena

3 tz. aceite para freír

2 | ¹/₂ lb. (225g) en total: cebolla, pimiento verde, zanahoria y tomate, todo cortado en pedazos (Fig. 1)

1 C. ajo finamente picado

3 | ²/₃ c. sal
3 C. c/u: azúcar, vinagre, ketchup
1 ¹/₂ C. maicena
6 C. agua

2 tz. arroz cocido

---

1. Corte la carne en rebanadas en grosor de 2/3" (1.5 cm); ablándela con un machacador (Fig. 2). Luego corte en pedazos de 1" (2.5 cm); mezcle bien con **1** . Ponga la carne y la maicena en una bolsa de plástico; agite la bolsa para rebozar la carne completamente (Fig. 3).

2. Caliente aceite para freír. Agregue los pedazos de carne uno por uno (Fría en dos partes si el aceite no cubre la carne); fría los pedazos de carne a fuego alto por 2 minutos hasta que estén cocidos y crujientes. Retire.

3. Caliente 1 C. de aceite. Agregue **2** y 1 C. de agua; fría-revolviendo brevemente luego retire. Limpie la sartén wok; caliente 2 C. de aceite. Fría-revolviendo el ajo hasta que esté aromático; agregue la mezcla **3** y haga hervir. Agregue los pedazos de carne y **2** ; fría-revolviendo hasta que se mezcle bien. Retire; coloque sobre el arroz y sirva con vegetales.

■ Los pedazos de carne se pueden freír y luego congelar por adelantado. Cuando los necesite, hornee por 10 minutos en el horno precalentado a 450°F (230°C).

Beef & Black Beans Over Rice
Carne de Res y Frijoles Negros Sobre Arroz

豆豉湘牛飯

- Serves 2 -

$^2/_3$ lb. (300g) lean beef, sliced
(Fig. 1)

1
1 T. soy sauce
1 T. cooking wine
2 T. water
$^1/_4$ t. baking soda

1 egg white (small)
1 T. cornstarch
1 T. oil

2
3 garlic cloves, sliced
$^1/_4$ c. ginger, sliced
$^1/_4$ c. red bell pepper, sliced
1 t. fermented black beans
(rinsed)

6 green onion sections (white
part), 2" (5 cm) long

3
1 t. each: sugar, cornstarch,
sesame oil
$^1/_2$ T. dark soy sauce (Fig. 2)
3 T. water

6 green onion sections (green
part), 2" (5 cm) long
2 c. cooked rice

1   Mix beef with **1** ; add egg white,
    cornstarch then oil; mix well.

2   Heat 4 T. oil. Stir-fry beef until
    almost cooked; remove. Use
    remaining oil to stir-fry **2** (Fig. 3)
    and white part of green onion until
    fragrant. Add mixture **3** , green
    part of green onion, and meat;
    stir-fry to mix well.

3   Put rice on 2 serving plates, and
    top with the beef and serve with
    vegetables.

■   Chili pepper may be added in **2**
    if desired.

- 2人份 -

牛瘦肉（切片，圖1）
 ·········· 半斤（300公克）

1
醬油 ··········1大匙
酒 ··········1大匙
水 ··········2大匙
小蘇打 ··········$^1/_4$小匙

蛋白（小的）··········1個
玉米粉 ··········1大匙
油 ··········1大匙

2
蒜（切片）··········3瓣
薑（切片）··········$^1/_4$杯
紅椒（切片）··········$^1/_4$杯
豆豉（略洗）··········1小匙

蔥白（5公分長）··········6段

3
糖、玉米粉、麻油 ···各1小匙
老抽（深色醬油，圖2）
 ··········$^1/_2$大匙
水 ··········3大匙

蔥綠（5公分長）··········6段

飯 ··········2碗

1   牛肉先調 **1** 料，再入蛋白、玉
    米粉及油拌勻。

2   油4大匙燒熱，入牛肉炒約九
    分熟撈出，餘油將 **2** 料（圖3）
    及蔥白炒香，再加調勻的 **3**
    料、蔥綠及肉炒拌均勻即成。

3   盤內盛飯，上置炒好的牛肉與
    蔬菜配食。

■   喜食辣者，可在 **2** 料內加辣
    椒。

- 2 porciones -

$^2/_3$ lb. (300g) carne de res,
rebanada (Fig. 1)

1
1 C. salsa de soya
1 C. vino para cocinar
2 C. agua
$^1/_4$ c. bicarbonato

1 clara de huevo (chico)
1 C. maicena
1 C. aceite

2
3 dientes de ajo, rebanados
$^1/_4$ tz. jengibre, rebanado
$^1/_4$ tz. pimiento rojo,
rebanado
1 c. frijoles negros
fermentados (enjuagados)

6 pedazos de cebollín (parte
blanca), 2" (5 cm) de
largo

3
1 c. c/u: azúcar, maicena,
aceite de sésamo
$^1/_2$ C. salsa de soya oscura
(Fig. 2)
3 C. agua

6 pedazos de cebollín (parte
verde), 2" (5 cm) de largo
2 tz. arroz cocido

1   Mezcle la carne con **1** ; agregue la
    clara de huevo, maicena, luego el
    aceite; mezcle bien.

2   Caliente 4 C. de aceite. Fría-
    revolviendo la carne hasta que esté
    casi cocida; retire. Use el aceite
    restante para freír-revolviendo **2**
    (Fig. 3) y la parte blanca del
    cebollín hasta que esté aromático.
    Agregue la mezcla **3** , la parte
    verde del cebollín, y la carne; fría-
    revolviendo hasta mezclar bien.

3   Divida el arroz en los 2 platos a
    servir, cubra con la carne y sirva
    con vegetales.

■   Si gusta puede usar chile en **2** .

Spicy Seafood & Meat Over Rice
Mariscos y Carne Picante Sobre Arroz

宮保三鮮飯

1

2

3

- Serves 2 -

1 Total of ¹/₂ lb. (225g): squid, lean meat (pork, beef or chicken) & shrimp

2 ¹/₄ t. salt
1 t. cornstarch

3 1 c. asparagus, sectioned
1 c. mushrooms, sliced
6 slices red bell pepper

4 3 garlic cloves, sliced
5 dried chili peppers, sliced
¹/₂ c. green onion sections
  (white part), 2" (5 cm) long

5 1 t. each: sugar, vinegar, sesame oil
1 T. cooking wine
1 T. soy sauce
¹/₂ T. dark soy sauce
  (see p. 12, Fig. 2)
¹/₂ T. cornstarch
2 T. water
¹/₂ c. green onion sections
  (green part), 2" (5 cm) long

2 c. cooked rice

- 2人份 -

1 魷魚、瘦肉（豬、牛或鷄）、
  蝦仁……共6兩（225公克）

2 鹽 ……………………¹/₄小匙
玉米粉 …………………1小匙

3 蘆筍（切段）……………1杯
毛菇（切片）……………1杯
紅椒 ………………………6片

4 蒜（切片）………………3瓣
乾辣椒（略切）…………5條
蔥白（5公分長）………¹/₂杯

5 糖 ………………………1小匙
醋 ………………………1小匙
麻油 ……………………1小匙
酒 ………………………1大匙
醬油 ……………………1大匙
老抽(深色醬油見12頁，圖2)
  …………………………¹/₂大匙
玉米粉 …………………¹/₂大匙
水 ………………………2大匙
蔥綠（5公分長）………¹/₂杯

飯 ………………………2碗

- 2 porciones -

1 ¹/₂ lb. (225g) en total: calamar, carne magra de cerdo, res o pollo y camarones

2 ¹/₄ c. sal
1 c. maicena

3 1 tz. espárragos en secciones
1 tz. hongos, rebanados
6 torrejas de pimiento rojo

4 3 dientes de ajo, rebanados
5 chiles secos, rebanados
¹/₂ tz. cebollín cortado a lo largo de 2" (5 cm) (parte blanca)

5 1 c. c/u: azúcar, vinagre, aceite de sésamo
1 C. vino para cocinar
1 C. salsa de soya
¹/₂ C. salsa de soya oscura
  (vea p. 12, Fig. 2)
¹/₂ C. maicena
2 C. agua
¹/₂ tz. cebollín cortado a lo largo de 2" (5 cm) (parte verde)

2 tz. arroz cocido

---

1 Score the squid of **1** in a crisscross manner (Fig. 1) then cut in pieces (see p. 21, Fig. 1). Slice meat; mix meat and shrimp well with **2**.

2 Heat 1 T. oil. Add **3** (Fig. 2) and 1 T. water; cover and cook until steamy. Stir-fry briefly; remove. Wipe wok dry.

3 Heat 3 T. oil. Add **4** (Fig. 3); stir-fry until garlic turns brown. Add **1** and stir-fry until separated and cooked. Add mixture **5** and **3**; stir-fry to mix well. Place on top of rice and serve.

---

1 將 **1** 料（圖1）內的魷魚切花（見21頁，圖1），肉切片與蝦仁調 **2** 料拌勻。

2 油1大匙燒熱，入 **3** 料（圖2）及水1大匙蓋鍋見水蒸氣冒出後略炒鏟出，擦乾鍋面。

3 油3大匙燒熱，放入 **4** 料（圖3）炒至蒜呈金黃色，再入 **1** 料炒開至熟，並加調勻的 **5** 料及炒好的 **3** 料炒拌均勻置於飯上即成。

---

1 Haga cortes a los calamares de **1** en forma de cruz (Fig. 1) luego corte en pedazos (vea p. 21, Fig. 1). Rebane la carne; mezcle bien la carne y camarones con **2**.

2 Caliente 1 C. de aceite. Agregue **3** (Fig. 2) y 1 C. de agua; tape y cocine hasta que evapore. Fría-revolviendo brevemente; retire. Seque la sartén wok.

3 Caliente 3 C. de aceite. Agregue **4** (Fig. 3); fría-revolviendo hasta que el ajo se dore. Agregue **1** y fría-revolviendo hasta que la carne esté separada y cocida. Agregue la mezcla **5** y **3**; fría-revolviendo para mezclar bien. Acomode arriba del arroz y sirva.

Beef & Beans Over Rice

Carne de Res y Frijoles Sobre Arroz

乾扁牛肉飯

1

2

3

²/₃ lb. (300g) beef (shredded, Fig. 1)

1 | ³/₄ T. cooking wine
³/₄ T. soy sauce
1 ¹/₃ T. cornstarch
pepper as desired

2 | Total of ¹/₂ lb. (225g), shredded (Fig. 2): string beans, celery and carrots

3 | ¹/₂ T. sugar
¹/₂ T. cooking wine
1 ¹/₂ T. soy sauce
1 t. hot bean paste (Fig. 3) or chili paste
1 t. sesame oil

2 c. cooked rice

1 Mix beef with **1** well.

2 Heat 4 T. oil in a non-stick pan. Fry beef 6 minutes until dried and brown; remove. Place meat on paper towel to absorb oil.

3 Heat 1 T. oil. Add **2** and 1 T. water; cover and cook until steamy; stir-fry briefly until sauce evaporates. Add in beef and mixture **3**; stir-fry to mix well.

4 Put rice on 2 serving plates, and top with the beef and vegetable mixture.

牛肉（切絲，圖1）
　　…………半斤（300公克）

1 | 酒 ………………………³/₄大匙
醬油 ……………………³/₄大匙
玉米粉 …………………1 ¹/₃大匙
胡椒 ………………………少許

2 | 四季豆、芹菜、紅蘿蔔切絲
（圖2）…共6兩（225公克）

3 | 糖 ………………………¹/₂大匙
酒 ………………………¹/₂大匙
醬油 ……………………1 ¹/₂大匙
辣豆瓣醬（圖3）或辣椒醬
　　………………………1小匙
麻油 ……………………1小匙

飯 ………………………2碗

1 牛肉調 **1** 料拌勻。

2 油4大匙燒熱，入牛肉半煎炸至水份爆出，肉呈褐色即撈出（約6分鐘），置於紙巾上吸油。

3 油1大匙燒熱，入 **2** 料及水1大匙蓋鍋見水蒸氣冒出後略炒至汁收乾，鑹於鍋邊；放入牛肉及調勻的 **3** 料炒勻，再入鍋邊的 **2** 料拌合置於飯上。

■ 此菜的牛肉原本是用炸的，但爲考慮家庭方便，牛肉可改用煎炸的方式，建議使用不粘鍋，且油量不要少於4大匙。

---

²/₃ lb. (300g) carne de res (desmenuzada, Fig. 1)

1 | ³/₄ C. vino para cocinar
³/₄ C. salsa de soya
1 ¹/₃ C. maicena
pimienta a gusto

2 | ¹/₂ lb. (225g) en total: frijoles verdes, apio, zanahoria, todo cortado (Fig. 2)

3 | ¹/₂ C. azúcar
¹/₂ C. vino para cocinar
1 ¹/₂ C. salsa de soya
1 c. salsa de frijol picante (Fig. 3) o pasta de chile
1 c. aceite de sésamo

2 tz. arroz cocido

1 Mezcle bien la carne con **1**.

2 Caliente 4 C. de aceite en una sartén que no se pegue. Fría la carne por 6 minutos hasta que esté seca y dorada; retire. Ponga la carne en toalla de papel para absorber el aceite.

3 Caliente 1 C. de aceite. Agregue **2** y 1 C. de agua; tape y cocine hasta evaporar; fría-revolviendo hasta que la salsa se evapore. Agregue la carne y la mixtura **3**; fría-revolviendo para mezclar bien.

4 Ponga el arroz en 2 platos a servir, acomode arriba la carne y la mezcla de vegetales.

Golden Gate Fried Rice
Arroz Frito Golden Gate

金門炒飯

1

2

3

- Serves 2 -

$^1/_3$ lb. (150g) bok choy (Fig. 1) or Taiwan bok choy (Fig. 2)

2 Chinese sausages* (Fig. 3), sliced

2 eggs (beaten)

2 c. cooked rice

1 | $^1/_4$ t. salt
| $^1/_8$ t. pepper

1 T. chopped green onions

---

1 Bring 4 c. water to boil. Add 1/2 t. salt, 1/2 T. oil and vegetables; bring to another boil. Remove the vegetables and plunge in cold water until cool. Squeeze out water, mince; and set aside.

2 Heat 1 T. oil. Stir-fry sausages over medium heat until oil is released; remove. Wipe wok dry.

3 Heat 2 T. oil. Add eggs and stir-fry until they solidify. Add rice and **1** ; stir-fry to mix well. Add vegetables, sausages and onions; stir-fry and mix well.

★ Other types of sausage or lean meat (marinated before using) may be used for Chinese sausages.

- 2人份 -

青江菜（圖1）或小白菜（圖2）
……………4兩（150公克）

中式香腸＊（圖3，切片）2條

蛋（打散）……………2個

飯 ……………2碗

1 | 鹽 ……………$^1/_4$小匙
| 胡椒 ……………$^1/_8$小匙

蔥花 ……………1大匙

---

1 水4杯燒開，放入鹽$^1/_2$小匙、油$^1/_2$大匙及青菜再燒開後撈出，放入冷水內漂涼，擠乾水份，切碎備用。

2 油1大匙燒熱，入香腸以中火炒至出油後撈出，擦乾鍋面。

3 油2大匙燒熱，入蛋液輕炒拌至凝固，隨入飯及 **1** 料炒勻，再加青菜、香腸及蔥花炒拌均勻即成。

★ 中式香腸可用其他種類的香腸或瘦肉（略醃後使用）取代。

- 2 porciones -

$^1/_3$ lb. (150g) bok choy (Fig. 1) o bok choy taiwanés (Fig. 2)

2 salchichas chinas* (Fig. 3), rebanadas

2 huevos batidos

2 tz. arroz cocido

1 | $^1/_4$ c. sal
| $^1/_8$ c. pimienta

1 C. cebollín picado

---

1 Haga hervir 4 tz. de agua. Agregue 1/2 c. sal, 1/2 C. de aceite y los vegetales; déles otro hervor. Retire los vegetales y sumérjalos en agua fría para enfriar. Estruje el agua, corte finamente; deje aparte.

2 Caliente 1 C. de aceite. Fría-revolviendo las salchichas a fuego moderado hasta que suelten el aceite; retire. Seque la sartén wok.

3 Caliente 2 C. de aceite. Agregue los huevos y fría-revolviendo hasta que se cuajen. Agregue el arroz y **1** ; fría-revolviendo para mezclar bien. Agregue los vegetales, salchichas y cebolla; fría-revolviendo y mezcle bien.

★ Se puede usar otras clases de salchichas o carne magra (marinada antes de usar) en lugar de salchichas chinas.

Fried Dumplings
Masitas Rellenas Fritas

鍋貼

1

2

3

²/₃ lb. (300g) ground pork (Fig. 1)

1
| ¹/₄ t. black pepper
| 1 T. cooking wine
| 1 T. sesame oil
| 3 T. each: soy sauce, water

1 lb. (450g) bok choy or Taiwanese bok choy (see p. 18, Figs. 1 & 2)
¹/₂ c. bamboo shoots (fresh or canned, minced)
¹/₂ c. Chinese black mushrooms (presoftened in cold water, minced)
1 c. yellow Chinese chives, (Fig. 2, minced)
50 sheets dumpling skin (Fig. 3)

1 Mix ground pork with **1** well. Blanch vegetables in hot water briefly; remove and plunge in cold water to cool. Squeeze out water then mince.

2 Heat 2 T. oil. Stir-fry bamboo shoots until yellow. Add mushrooms and stir-fry until fragrant; remove and let cool. Mix well with pork, vegetables and chives to make filling.

3 Place filling in center of each dumpling skin; fold in the two ends and seal the edges with water.

4 Heat 1 T. oil in a non-stick pan; arrange half the dumplings in a pan (fry them in batches). Fry until dumpling bottoms turn brown; pour in 1/2 c. water. Cover and cook over medium heat 6 minutes. Uncover and continue to cook until water evaporates; invert on a plate and serve. May be served with rice.

■ Uncooked dumplings may be frozen. To fry the frozen dumplings, arrange the dumplings in a non-stick pan, pour in 3/4 c. water, cover and cook over medium heat 10 minutes. Other procedures are the same as step 4.

豬絞肉（圖1）
　　　　……半斤（300公克）

1
| 胡椒 ················¹/₄小匙
| 酒 ··················1大匙
| 麻油 ················1大匙
| 醬油 ················3大匙
| 水 ·················3大匙

青江菜或小白菜（見18頁，圖
　1、2）……12兩（450公克）
筍（新鮮或罐頭、切碎）···¹/₂杯
香菇（泡軟、切碎）······¹/₂杯
韭菜（圖2，切碎）·········1杯
餃子皮（圖3）·······約50張

1 絞肉調 **1** 料拌勻。青菜在滾水內略燙撈出，用冷水漂涼，擠乾水份，切碎備用。

2 油2大匙燒熱，先將筍炒至淡黃色，隨後香菇炒香後撈出，待涼後與絞肉、青菜及韭菜全部攪拌成餡。

3 將餡放在皮中央，皮外圍塗少許水折半捏緊。

4 不黏的平底鍋內，入油1大匙將鍋貼依序排入（分二次煎）煎至底部呈淡黃色，淋入水¹/₂杯，蓋鍋用中火煮約6分鐘，打開鍋蓋續煮至水乾，倒扣置盤即可。可單獨吃或與飯共食。

■ 鍋貼可冷凍，煎時直接放入平底鍋內，淋水³/₄杯，燜煮時間改爲10分鐘。其他作法同 4 。

---

²/₃ lb. (300g) carne molida de cerdo (Fig. 1)

1
| ¹/₄ c. pimienta negra
| 1 C. vino para cocinar
| 1 C. aceite de sésamo
| 3 C. c/u: salsa de soya, agua

1 lb. (450g) bok choy o bok choy taiwanés (vea p. 18, Figs. 1 & 2)
¹/₂ tz. retoños de bambú (frescos o enlatados, finamente picados)
¹/₂ tz. hongos negros chinos (remojados previamente en agua fría, finamente picados)
1 tz. cebollín amarillo chino (Fig. 2, finamente picado)
50 hojitas de masa (Fig. 3)

1 Mezcle bien la carne molida de cerdo con **1** . Escalde brevemente los vegetales en agua caliente; sáquelos y sumerja en agua fría para enfriar. Estrújeles el agua y píquelos finamente.

2 Caliente 2 C. de aceite. Fría-revolviendo los retoños de bambú hasta que se pongan amarillos. Agregue los hongos y fría-revolviendo hasta que esté aromático; retire y deje enfriar. Mezcle bien con la carne, vegetales y cebollines para hacer el relleno.

3 Ponga el relleno en el centro de cada hoja de masa, doble en los extremos y selle las orillas con agua.

4 Caliente 1 C. de aceite en una sartén que no se pegue; acomode la mitad de las masitas en la sartén (fríalas en grupos). Fríalas hasta que la parte de abajo se dore; écheles 1/2 tz. de agua. Tape y cocine a fuego moderado por 6 minutos. Destape y continúe cocinando hasta que el agua se evapore; inviértalas en un plato y sirva. Puede servir con arroz.

■ Las masitas sin cocinar se pueden congelar. Para freír las masitas congeladas, acomódelas en una sartén que no se pegue, agregue 3/4 tz. de agua, tape y cocine a fuego moderado por 10 minutos. Continúe el mismo procedimiento del paso 4.

Spicy Seafood Noodles
Fideos con Mariscos Picantes

三鮮湯馬麵

1

2

3

- Serves 2 -

1 Total of ¹/₂ lb. (225g): squid (score crisscross then cut in pieces, Fig. 1), shelled shrimp, lean meat (shredded pork, beef or chicken)

2 3 dried chili peppers (Fig. 2), cut in pieces
2 T. dried shrimp
¹/₂ T. minced garlic

1 T. soy sauce

3 1 c. shredded onion
1 c. pre-softened Chinese wood ears, shredded
Total of ¹/₃ lb. (150g), shredded: cabbage, carrot and other vegetables

4 2 T. paprika (Fig. 3)
¹/₂ t. salt
1 t. each: sugar, cooking wine
2 c. canned chicken broth
2 c. water

¹/₃ lb. (150g) dry noodles

1 Heat 2 T. oil. Stir-fry **1** until cooked; remove.

2 Heat 2 T. oil. Stir-fry **2** over medium heat until brown; add soy sauce and **3** ; stir-fry briefly. Add **4** ; bring to boil. Add **1** to complete the soup; remove.

3 Follow instructions on package to cook noodles. Divide noodles into 2 serving bowls and pour in the soup. Serve.

■ Lean meat may be used for **1** . This is a famous spicy dish in northern China. Chili peppers in **2** may be increased or decreased according to personal preference.

- 2人份 -

1 魷魚（切花，圖1）、蝦仁、瘦肉（豬、牛或鷄切絲）
⋯⋯⋯⋯⋯⋯共6兩（225公克）

2 乾辣椒（圖2，略切）⋯⋯⋯3條
蝦米⋯⋯⋯⋯⋯⋯⋯⋯⋯2大匙
蒜（切碎）⋯⋯⋯⋯⋯⋯¹/₂大匙

醬油⋯⋯⋯⋯⋯⋯⋯⋯⋯1大匙

3 洋蔥（切絲）⋯⋯⋯⋯⋯⋯1杯
泡軟木耳（切絲）⋯⋯⋯⋯1杯
白菜（或高麗菜）、紅蘿蔔
⋯⋯⋯切絲共4兩（150公克）

4 紅椒粉（圖3）⋯⋯⋯⋯⋯2大匙
鹽⋯⋯⋯⋯⋯⋯⋯⋯⋯¹/₂小匙
糖、酒⋯⋯⋯⋯⋯⋯各1小匙
罐頭鷄湯＊（內含鹽）⋯⋯2杯
水⋯⋯⋯⋯⋯⋯⋯⋯⋯⋯2杯

乾麵⋯⋯⋯⋯⋯4兩（150公克）

1 油2大匙燒熱，將 **1** 料炒開至熟撈出。

2 油2大匙用中小火將 **2** 料炒至蒜呈金黃色，隨入醬油及 **3** 料略炒再加 **4** 料燒開，最後放入炒好的 **1** 料即成三鮮湯。

3 多量水燒開，依包裝指示將麵煮熟，撈出分盛碗內，加入三鮮湯即成。

＊ 若使用一般自製高湯可酌加鹽³/₄小匙。

■ **1** 料內的材料，可全部用瘦肉（豬、牛或鷄）共6兩（225公克），此菜餚為北方有名的辣味麵食， **2** 料內的乾辣椒可隨意加多或減少。

- 2 porciones -

1 ¹/₂ lb. (225g) en total: calamares (con cortes cruzados y luego cortados en pedazos, Fig. 1), camarones pelados, carne magra (cerdo, res o pollo, desmenuzado)

2 3 chiles secos (Fig. 2) cortados en pedazos
2 C. camarones secos
¹/₂ C. ajo finamente picado

1 C. salsa de soya

3 1 tz. cebolla picada
1 tz. orejas de madera chinas, remojadas previamente, picadas
¹/₃ lb. (150g) en total picados: repollo, zanahoria y otros vegetales

4 2 C. pimentón (Fig. 3)
¹/₂ c. sal
1 c. c/u: azúcar, vino para cocinar
2 tz. caldo de pollo enlatado
2 tz. agua

¹/₃ lb. (150g) fideos secos

1 Caliente 2 C. de aceite. Fría-revolviendo **1** hasta que esté cocido; retire.

2 Caliente 2 C. de aceite. Fría-revolviendo **2** a fuego moderado hasta que se dore; agregue la salsa de soya y **3** ; fría-revolviendo brevemente. Agregue **4** ; haga hervir. Agregue **1** para completar la sopa; retire.

3 Para cocinar los fideos siga las instrucciones del paquete. Acomode los fideos en los dos tazones a servir y vacíe la sopa encima. Sirva.

■ Carne magra se puede usar en lugar de **1** . Este es un famoso platillo picante del norte de China. Puede aumentar o disminuir los chiles en **2** de acuerdo a su gusto.

Shrimp Fajitas
Fajitas de Camarones

墨式炒蝦

1

2

3

- Serves 2 -

1
- $^{1}/_{2}$ lb. (225g) medium-size raw shelled shrimp
- $^{1}/_{4}$ t. ea: salt, pepper, ground cumin, chili powder
- 1 t. finely diced dry cilantro* or parsley*
- 1 t. oil
- 1 T. lemon juice

2
- $^{1}/_{2}$ ea: medium size green, red, and yellow bell peppers
- $^{1}/_{2}$ medium onion

3
- 1 T. teriyaki sauce
- 1 medium tomato, cut in wedges

4 flour or corn tortillas, or cooked white rice

1 Devein shrimp, rinse and pat dry with paper towels. Mix **1** in bowl, add shrimp and marinate for 30 minutes (Fig. 1). Cut **2** length-wise and separate onion rings (Fig. 2).

2 Heat 2 T. oil in skillet over high heat, add **2**, fry until edges are lightly browned. Push to side of skillet, add shrimp and fry until cooked. Add **3** and mix with **2** and shrimp, saute 1/2 minute. Serve with warm tortillas or cooked white rice. When served with tortillas, salsa and sour cream go well with Fajitas.

★ 1 t. of finely diced dry herbs equals 1 T. of loosely packed finely diced fresh herbs.

■ 1/2 lb. (225g) boneless chicken breast or round steak cut into 2" (5 cm) strips can be substituted for shrimp (Fig. 3).

- 2人份 -

1
- 去殼中蝦 ⋯⋯6兩（225公克）
- 鹽、胡椒 ⋯⋯⋯⋯⋯各$^{1}/_{4}$小匙
- 辣椒粉 ⋯⋯⋯⋯⋯⋯$^{1}/_{4}$小匙
- 小茴香粉 ⋯⋯⋯⋯⋯$^{1}/_{4}$小匙
- 碎乾香菜或碎乾巴西利*1小匙
- 油 ⋯⋯⋯⋯⋯⋯⋯⋯1小匙
- 檸檬汁 ⋯⋯⋯⋯⋯⋯1大匙

2
- 青椒（中）⋯⋯⋯⋯⋯$^{1}/_{2}$個
- 紅椒（中）⋯⋯⋯⋯⋯$^{1}/_{2}$個
- 黃椒（中）⋯⋯⋯⋯⋯$^{1}/_{2}$個
- 洋蔥（中）⋯⋯⋯⋯⋯$^{1}/_{2}$個

3
- 串燒醬 **（Teriyaki Sauce）⋯⋯⋯⋯⋯⋯⋯⋯⋯⋯1大匙
- 番茄（中，切塊）⋯⋯⋯1個

麵粉薄餅、玉米薄餅或木須皮
4片或白飯 ⋯⋯⋯⋯⋯2碗

1 蝦去腸泥，洗淨後用紙巾吸乾水份，調入 **1** 料醃30分鐘（圖1）。將 **2** 料切條（圖2）。

2 油2大匙燒熱，入 **2** 料略炒鏟出，隨入蝦炒熟，再加炒好的 **2** 料、**3** 料炒30秒鐘與熱薄餅或飯配食。若用熱薄餅可加辣茄醬（見29頁）或酸奶油更美味。

★ 碎乾香菜或巴西利1小匙相當於新鮮切碎的香菜或巴西利1大匙。

** 如無串燒醬可用醬油1大匙，糖與酒各1小匙，太白粉$^{1}/_{3}$小匙拌勻來取代。

■ 喜食肉者，可用鷄胸肉或牛肉（切條，圖3）來取代蝦。

- 2 porciones -

1
- $^{1}/_{2}$ lb. (225g) camarones crudos, pelados
- $^{1}/_{4}$ c. c/u: sal, pimienta, comino molido, chile en polvo
- 1 c. cilantro o perejil seco finamente picado*
- 1 c. aceite
- 1 C. jugo de limón

2
- $^{1}/_{2}$ c/u: pimientos verdes, rojos y amarillos medianos
- $^{1}/_{2}$ cebolla mediana

3
- 1 C. salsa teriyaki
- 1 tomate mediano, cortado en rodajas

4 tortillas de harina o maíz, o arroz blanco cocido

1 Desvene los camarones, enjuague y séquelos ligeramente con toallas de papel. Mezcle **1** en un tazón, agregue los camarones y marine por 30 minutos (Fig. 1). Corte **2** a lo largo y separe las rodajas de la cebolla (Fig. 2).

2 Caliente 2 C. de aceite en una sartén a fuego alto, agregue **2**, fría hasta que las orillas estén ligeramente doradas. Hágalas a un lado de la sartén, agregue los camarones y fría hasta que estén cocidos. Agregue **3** y mezcle con **2** y los camarones, sofría por 1/2 minuto. Sirva con las tortillas calientes o con el arroz. Cuando se sirve con tortillas, este platillo se complementa con salsa y crema agria.

★ 1 c. de especias secas finamente picadas equivale a 1 C. de especias frescas finamente picadas.

■ En lugar de camarones se puede usar 1/2 lb. (225g) pechuga de pollo sin hueso o bistec redondo cortado en tiras de 2" (5 cm) (Fig. 3).

Chicken with Rice
Arroz con Pollo

鶏肉飯

- Serves 4 -

1 $^1/_2$ lbs. (675g) skinned
boneless chicken breasts

1
- $^1/_2$ c. $^1/_4$" (0.5 cm) diced onions
- 1 garlic clove, minced
- 1 c. raw long-grain rice

2
- 1 $^1/_2$ c. chopped tomatoes
- $^1/_2$ t. chili powder
- 1 t. salt
- $^1/_8$ t. pepper
- 2 c. canned ready-to-serve
  chicken broth

1 $^1/_2$ c. fresh or frozen peas

8 flour or corn tortillas

1. Wash chicken, pat dry, and cut into large bite-size pieces (Fig. 1). Heat 3 T. oil in deep pot over high heat. Fry chicken until lightly brown on all sides (Fig. 2). Remove chicken, add 2 T. oil if needed, add **1** and saute in juices over medium heat until rice is lightly brown (Fig. 3).

2. Add **2** and chicken to pot, mix well. Increase heat and bring to boil, lower heat, cover and simmer about 25 minutes until chicken is fully cooked and rice is tender. Add water if needed to keep rice moist.

3. Mix in peas, cook 5 more minutes until peas are tender. Serve with warm tortillas and salsa.

- 4人份 -

鶏胸肉（去皮）
........1斤2兩（675公克）

1
- 洋蔥（切丁）............$^1/_2$杯
- 蒜（切碎）.................1瓣
- 長米（再來米）.............1杯

2
- 番茄（切小塊）.......1 $^1/_2$杯
- 辣椒粉................$^1/_2$小匙
- 鹽....................1小匙
- 胡椒..................$^1/_8$小匙
- 罐頭鷄湯＊（內含鹽）......2杯

新鮮或冷凍靑豆仁......1 $^1/_2$杯

麵粉薄餅、玉米薄餅或木須皮
..............8片

1. 肉洗淨拭乾水份，切塊（圖1）。油3大匙燒熱，將肉兩面煎至金黃色（圖2）取出。

2. 如太乾加油2大匙，用中火將 **1** 料炒至米呈金黃色（圖3），隨入 **2** 料及煎好的肉拌勻用大火燒開，降低火候蓋鍋煮25分鐘至肉及米熟（如太乾略加水），再加靑豆仁拌炒至熟約5分鐘即成。

3. 鷄肉飯適合與熱薄餅及辣茄醬（見29頁）共食。

★ 若使用一般自製高湯可酌加鹽 $^3/_4$小匙。

■ 麵粉薄餅及玉米薄餅在美式超市可買到現成製品，若無，可用木須皮取代。

- 4 porciones -

1 $^1/_2$ lb. (675g) pechugas de
pollo sin hueso y sin piel

1
- $^1/_2$ tz. cebolla picada en
  cubitos de $^1/_4$" (0.5 cm)
- 1 diente de ajo, finamente
  picado
- 1 tz. arroz crudo de grano
  largo

2
- 1 $^1/_2$ tz. tomate picado
- $^1/_2$ c. chile en polvo
- 1 c. sal
- $^1/_8$ c. pimienta
- 2 tz. caldo de pollo enlatado,
  listo para servir

1 $^1/_2$ tz. chícharos frescos o
congelados

8 tortillas de harina o maíz

1. Lave el pollo, seque ligeramente, y corte en pedazos grandes tamaño bocado (Fig. 1). Caliente 3 C. de aceite en una olla honda a fuego alto. Fría el pollo hasta que esté un poco dorado por todos lados (Fig. 2). Retire el pollo, agregue 2 C. de aceite si es necesario, agregue **1** y sofría en su jugo a fuego mediano hasta que el arroz esté ligeramente dorado (Fig. 3).

2. Agregue **2** y el pollo a la olla, mezcle bien. Suba el fuego y haga hervir, baje el fuego, tape, cocine lentamente como por 25 minutos hasta que el pollo esté completamente cocido y el arroz esté tierno. Agregue agua si es necesario para mantener húmedo el arroz.

3. Agregue los chícharos, cocine por 5 minutos más hasta que los chícharos estén tiernos. Sirva con tortillas calientes y salsa.

Mexican Pork Chops
Chuletas de Cerdo a la Mexicana

烤豬排飯

1

2

3

- Serves 4 -

4 large (1 $^2/_3$ lb., 750g) pork chops

1. $^1/_2$ c. $^1/_4$" (0.5 cm) diced onions
   $^3/_4$ c. $^1/_4$" (0.5 cm) diced green bell peppers
   1 c. $^1/_2$" (1 cm) chopped tomatoes

2. 1 $^3/_4$ c. ea: canned undrained whole kernel corn, red kidney beans

3. $^1/_2$ c. raw long-grain rice
   1 t. ea: salt, chili powder
   $^1/_4$ t. pepper

8 flour or corn tortillas

1. Trim fat from pork chops (Fig. 1). Heat 1 T. oil in large skillet and brown pork on both sides about 5 minutes over high heat. Remove meat and drain grease. Add ❶ (Fig. 2), ❷ (Fig. 3), and ❸ to skillet, mix and bring to boil for 3 minutes.

2. Place pork chops in 11" x 7" (28 cm x 18 cm) lightly buttered baking dish. Spoon mixture from skillet over pork chops. Cover with foil and seal tightly. Bake in preheated oven at 350°F (180°C) 30 minutes, uncover and bake 10 more minutes until rice is cooked. Serve with warm tortillas. Home made or store bought salsa goes well with this dish.

- 4人份 -

大豬排4塊1斤4兩（750公克）

① 洋蔥（切丁）…………$^1/_2$杯
   青椒（切丁）…………$^3/_4$杯
   番茄（切丁）……………1杯

② 罐頭玉米粒（連汁）……1 $^3/_4$杯
   罐頭腰形紅豆（連汁）…1 $^3/_4$杯

③ 長米（再來米）…………$^1/_2$杯
   鹽 ……………………1小匙
   辣椒粉…………………1小匙
   胡椒…………………$^1/_4$小匙

麵粉薄餅、玉米薄餅或木須皮
……………………………8片

1. 豬排去除肥肉（圖1）。油1大匙燒熱，將豬排兩面各煎5分鐘呈金黃色即取出，平鋪在28公分×18公分塗有奶油的烤盤上。

2. 將 ① 料（圖2）、 ② 料（圖3）、 ③ 料拌勻燒開約3分鐘，倒於豬排上，用鋁箔紙蓋緊；烤箱燒熱，以350℉（180℃）烤30分鐘後，不蓋鋁箔紙續烤10分鐘至米熟，與熱薄餅、辣茄醬配食。

辣茄醬：將番茄（切丁）1$^1/_2$杯，洋蔥（切碎）$^1/_2$杯，香菜（切碎）2大匙，辣椒（切碎）4支，鹽、醋（或檸檬）各1小匙攪拌即成。若太乾可加水1-3大匙。辣茄醬的用途如同中國人使用辣椒醬，此簡易辣茄醬做法由 EVA TORRES 女士提供。

- 4 porciones -

4 (1 $^2/_3$ lb., 750g) chuletas grandes de cerdo

1. $^1/_2$ tz. cebolla picada en cuadritos de $^1/_4$" (0.5 cm)
   $^3/_4$ tz. pimiento verde picado en cuadritos de $^1/_4$" (0.5 cm)
   1 tz. tomate picado en pedazos de $^1/_2$" (1 cm)

2. 1 $^3/_4$ tz. c/u enlatado sin escurrir: granos de elote, frijoles rojos

3. $^1/_2$ tz. arroz crudo de grano largo
   1 c. c/u: sal, chile en polvo
   $^1/_4$ c. pimienta

8 tortillas de harina o maíz

1. Quite la gordura de la carne (Fig. 1). Caliente 1 C. de aceite en una cacerola grande y dore las chuletas por ambos lados como por 5 minutos a fuego alto. Retire la carne y escurra la grasa. Agregue ❶ (Fig. 2), ❷ (Fig. 3) y ❸ a la cacerola, mezcle y haga hervir por 3 minutos.

2. Coloque las chuletas en un recipiente de hornear de 11" x 7" (28 cm x 18 cm) engrasado ligeramente. Vacíe la mezcla de la cacerola a cucharadas sobre las chuletas. Tape con papel de aluminio y selle apretadamente. Cocine en un horno precalentado a 350°F (180°C) por 30 minutos, destape y cocine por 10 minutos más hasta que el arroz esté cocido. Sirva con tortillas calientes. Salsa hecha en casa o comprada complementa este platillo.

Green Chili
Chile Verde

青椒燉肉燴飯

1

2

3

- Serves 4 -

2 ¹/₄ lbs. (1015g) boneless
pork loin roast

1 | ¹/₂ c. canned diced green
chilies

2 | 1 ¹/₂ c. finely diced onions
1 c. finely diced green bell
peppers

3 | 1 t. ground cumin
2 t. finely diced dry oregano
leaves*
¹/₂ t. ea: salt, pepper
¹/₄ c. finely diced dry cilantro*
or parsley*
1 ¹/₄ c. water
1 ¹/₄ c. canned ready-to-serve
chicken broth

4 c. cooked white rice

- 4人份 -

豬肉 …1斤11兩（1015公克）

1 | 罐頭青椒（切丁）………¹/₂杯

2 | 洋蔥（切丁）………1 ¹/₂杯
青椒（切丁）……………1杯

3 | 小茴香粉 ……………1小匙
碎乾俄力崗香料* ……2小匙
鹽 ………………………¹/₂小匙
胡椒 ……………………¹/₂小匙
碎乾香菜或碎乾巴西利* …¹/₄杯
水 ………………………1 ¹/₄杯
罐頭雞湯**（內含鹽）…1 ¹/₄杯

白飯 ……………………4杯

- 4 porciones -

2 ¹/₄ lbs. (1015g) asado de
lomo de cerdo

1 | ¹/₂ tz. chiles verdes picados,
enlatados

2 | 1 ¹/₂ tz. cebolla finamente
picada
1 tz. pimiento verde
finamente picado

3 | 1 c. comino molido
2 c. hojas de orégano seco
finamente picado*
¹/₂ c. c/u: sal, pimienta
¹/₄ tz. cilantro o perejil seco
finamente picado*
1 ¹/₄ tz. c/u: agua, caldo de
pollo enlatado, listo para
servir

4 tz. arroz blanco cocido

---

1 Trim fat from meat leaving 1 2/3 lb. (750g) cut into bite-size pieces (Fig. 1). Heat 2 T. oil in deep pot over high heat, add meat and lightly brown on all sides. Remove meat, set aside, reduce heat, add **1** (Fig. 2) and **2** (Fig. 3) and saute in meat juice until soft.

2 Put meat and **3** in pot and mix thoroughly. Bring to boil, reduce heat, cover and simmer for 1 1/2 hours stirring occasionally until mixture thickens and meat is tender.

3 Prepare rice and serve with chili verde mixture on top of rice. For variety, serve on top of cooked egg noodles.

* 1 t. of finely diced dry herbs equals 1 T. loosely packed finely diced fresh herbs.

---

1 豬肉去除肥肉後剩1斤8兩（750公克），切塊（圖1）。

2 油2大匙燒熱，將肉兩面煎至金黃色取出，隨入 **1** 料（圖2）、**2** 料（圖3）略炒，再加肉及 **3** 料燒開，略降火候蓋鍋煮90分鐘（中途需翻拌）至濃稠狀且肉熟軟。

3 將煮好的青椒燉肉澆在白飯或麵上即可食用。

* 碎乾香菜或巴西利1小匙相當於新鮮切碎的香菜或巴西利1大匙。

** 若使用一般自製高湯可酌加鹽1小匙。

■ 罐頭青椒是以加州特產長青椒去皮所製成（略有辣味），若無，亦可用一般青椒略加辣椒取代。

---

1 Quite la gordura de la carne dejando 1 2/3 lb. (750g), corte en pedazos tamaño bocado (Fig. 1). Caliente 2 C. de aceite en una olla honda a fuego alto, agregue la carne y dore ligeramente por todos lados. Retire la carne, deje aparte, baje el fuego, agregue **1** (Fig. 2) y **2** (Fig. 3) y sofría en el jugo de la carne hasta que se ablande.

2 Coloque la carne y **3** en la olla y mezcle completamente. Haga hervir, baje el fuego, tape y cocine lentamente por 1 1/2 horas revolviendo ocasionalmente hasta que la mezcla se espese y la carne esté tierna.

3 Prepare el arroz y sirva con la mezcla de chile verde sobre arroz. Como variedad, sirva sobre tallarines cocidos.

* 1 c. de hierbas secas finamente picadas equivale a 1 C. de hierbas frescas finamente picadas.

Tamale Casserole
Guiso de Tamales

玉米粉碎肉烤盅

1

2

3

- Serves 4 -	- 4人份 -	- 4 porciones -

1
- 1 lb. (450g) ground beef
- 1/2 c. 1/4" (0.5 cm) diced onions
- 3/4 c. 1/4" (0.5 cm) diced green bell peppers

2
- 1/4 t. salt
- 1/4 t. ground cumin
- 2 t. chili powder
- 1 c. tomato sauce
- 1 c. canned whole kernel corn, drained
- 1/2 c. sliced black olives

- 3/4 c. shredded cheddar cheese

3
- 1/4 t. salt
- 1/2 c. yellow corn meal (Fig. 1)
- 1 1/2 c. cold water

1 T. margarine or butter

1
- 牛絞肉 ……12兩（450公克）
- 洋蔥（切碎）……………1/2杯
- 靑椒（切碎）……………3/4杯

2
- 鹽 ………………………1/4小匙
- 小茴香粉 ………………1/4小匙
- 辣椒粉 …………………2小匙
- 番茄調味汁 ……………1杯
- 罐頭玉米粒（瀝汁）………1杯
- 黑橄欖（切片）…………1/2杯

- 巧達起士絲 ……………3/4杯

3
- 鹽 ………………………1/4小匙
- 玉米粗粉（圖1）………1/2杯
- 冷水 ……………………1 1/2杯

乳瑪琳或奶油 …………1大匙

1
- 1 lb. (450g) carne molida de res
- 1/2 tz. cebolla picada en cubitos de 1/4" (0.5 cm)
- 3/4 tz. pimiento verde picado en cubitos de 1/4" (0.5 cm)

2
- 1/4 c. sal
- 1/4 c. comino molido
- 2 c. chile en polvo
- 1 tz. salsa de tomate
- 1 tz. granos de elote enlatados, escurridos
- 1/2 tz. aceitunas negras en rebanadas

- 3/4 tz. queso Cheddar rallado

3
- 1/4 c. sal
- 1/2 tz. harina de maíz amarilla (Fig. 1)
- 1 1/2 tz. agua fría

1 C. margarina o mantequilla

---

1 Place **1** in deep pot over medium heat. Break up meat while frying. Fry until meat is brown. Drain off grease.

2 Add **2** to pot, mix thoroughly with meat mixture (Fig. 2) and simmer uncovered 15 minutes stirring occasionally until thick. Add shredded cheese, stir until melted. Pour into a 2-quart 8" x 8" (21 cm x 21 cm) baking dish.

3 Prepare crust by placing **3** in a pot. Cook over medium heat, stir until thick. Add butter, mix well. Spread crust mixture over meat mixture (Fig. 3). Bake uncovered in preheated oven 400°F (200°C) 30 minutes until crust is golden. Vegetables go well with this dish.

1 將 **1** 料放入無油無水的鍋內，用中火炒開至肉變色倒出油。

2 隨入 **2** 料與肉拌勻（圖2）不蓋鍋中火煮15分鐘至濃稠狀（中途需翻拌），再加起士攪至溶化，倒入21公分×21公分的烤盤內。

3 將 **3** 料拌勻，邊煮邊攪至濃稠狀，拌入奶油，澆在煮好的肉上（圖3）。烤箱燒熱，不加蓋以400℉（200℃）烤30分鐘至表面呈金黃色即成。可與蔬菜配食。

■ 玉米粗粉可在一般美式超市擺麵粉的架上找到。巧達起士色黃，市面有現成已切絲的，若一次用不完，可冰凍慢慢使用。

1 Coloque **1** en una olla honda a fuego moderado. Desbarate la carne mientras se cocina. Fría hasta que la carne esté dorada. Escurra la grasa.

2 Agregue **2** a la olla, mezcle completamente con la mezcla de carne (Fig. 2) y cocine destapada lentamente por 15 minutos revolviendo ocasionalmente hasta que se espese. Agregue el queso rallado, revuelva hasta que se derrita. Vacíe en un recipiente de hornear de 2 litros 8" x 8" (21 cm x 21 cm).

3 Prepare la masa poniendo **3** en una olla. Cocine a fuego moderado, revuelva hasta que espese. Agregue la mantequilla, mezcle bien. Extienda la masa sobre la mezcla de carne (Fig. 3). Hornee sin tapar en un horno precalentado a 400°F (200°C) por 30 minutos hasta que la masa esté dorada. Este platillo se completamenta con vegetales.

Enchilada Casserole
Guiso de Enchiladas

薄餅碎肉烤盅

1

2

3

- Serves 4 -

9 8" (21 cm) corn tortillas

1 | 1 lb. (450g) ground beef
  | $^3/_4$ c. ea: $^1/_4$" diced onions, green bell peppers

2 | 1 t. salt
  | $^1/_8$ t. ea: pepper, ground cumin
  | 1$^1/_2$ t. chili powder
  | 1 c. sliced black olives
  | 2$^1/_4$ c. tomato sauce
  | 1 c. water
  | 1 T. corn starch

1$^3/_4$ c. shredded cheddar cheese

- 4人份 -

玉米薄餅（直徑21公分）9片

1 | 牛絞肉 ……12兩（450公克）
  | 洋蔥（切丁）…………$^3/_4$杯
  | 青椒（切丁）…………$^3/_4$杯

2 | 鹽 …………………1小匙
  | 胡椒 ……………$^1/_8$小匙
  | 小茴香粉 ………$^1/_8$小匙
  | 辣椒粉 …………1$^1/_2$小匙
  | 黑橄欖（切片）………1杯
  | 番茄調味汁 ………2$^1/_4$杯
  | 水 ………………………1杯
  | 玉米粉 …………………1大匙

巧達起士絲 …………1$^3/_4$杯

- 4 porciones -

9 tortillas de maíz de 8" (21 cm)

1 | 1 lb. (450g) carne molida de res
  | $^3/_4$ tz. c/u: pimientos verdes, cebolla picada en cubitos de $^1/_4$" (0.5 cm)

2 | 1 c. sal
  | $^1/_8$ c. c/u: pimienta, comino molido
  | 1 $^1/_2$ c. chile en polvo
  | 1 tz. aceitunas negras rebanadas
  | 2 $^1/_4$ tz. salsa de tomate
  | 1 tz. agua
  | 1 C. maicena

1 $^3/_4$ tz. queso Cheddar rallado

---

1 Cut tortillas into wedges (Fig. 1), set aside. Place 1 in skillet over medium heat. Break up meat while frying (Fig. 2). Fry until meat is brown. Drain off grease, set aside.

2 Mix 2 in bowl until well blended. Add meat mixture, tortilla wedges and cheese; mix thoroughly. Pour into 2-quart 8" x 8" (21 cm x 21 cm) baking dish (Fig. 3) and bake uncovered in preheated oven 350°F (180°C) 25 minutes. Vegetables go well with this dish.￫

1 薄餅切成八等份（圖1）備用；將 1 料放入無油無水的鍋內用中火炒開（圖2）至肉變色熄火，倒出油。

2 2 料、薄餅及起士放入鍋內與炒好的肉混合均勻，倒入21公分×21公分的烤盤內（圖3）。烤箱燒熱，不加蓋以350℉（180℃）烤25分鐘即成。可與蔬菜配食。

■ 玉米薄餅是玉米麵粉（玉米細粉）、鹽及溫水揉合製成的薄餅，詳細做法見墨西哥菜第14頁。

1 Corte las tortillas en triángulos (Fig. 1), deje aparte. Ponga 1 en una cacerola a fuego moderado. Desbarate la carne mientras se fríe (Fig. 2). Fría hasta que la carne esté dorada. Escúrrale la grasa y deje aparte.

2 Mezcle 2 en un tazón hasta que esté bien revuelto. Agregue la mezcla de carne, tortillas y queso; mezcle completamente. Vacíe en un recipiente de hornear de 2 litros 8" x 8" (21 cm x 21 cm) (Fig. 3) y cocine destapado en un horno precalentado a 350°F (180°C) por 25 minutos. Este platillo se complementa con vegetales.

El Zorro's Chili
Chili de El Zorro

茄醬碎肉

1

2

3

- Serves 4 -	- 4人份 -	- 4 porciones -

1

1 lb. (450g) chili meat* or ground beef (Fig. 1)	粗牛絞瘦肉或牛絞肉＊（圖1）⋯⋯⋯⋯⋯12兩（450公克）	1 lb. (450g) carne tipo chili* o carne molida de res (Fig. 1)
$1/2$ c. ea: $1/4$" (0.5 cm) diced onions, green bell peppers (Fig. 2)	洋蔥（切丁，圖2）⋯⋯⋯$1/2$杯 青椒（切丁，圖2）⋯⋯⋯$1/2$杯	$1/2$ tz. c/u: cebolla, pimiento verde cortado en cubos de $1/4$" (0.5 cm) (Fig. 2)
1 garlic clove, minced	蒜（切碎）⋯⋯⋯⋯⋯⋯1瓣	1 diente de ajo, finamente picado

2

1 c. tomato sauce	番茄調味汁⋯⋯⋯⋯⋯1杯	1 tz. salsa de tomate
2 chopped tomatoes	番茄（切小塊）⋯⋯⋯⋯2個	2 tomates picados
$1^3/4$ c. ea: canned, undrained, red kidney beans, pinto beans (Fig. 3)	罐頭腰形紅豆（連汁，圖3）⋯⋯⋯⋯⋯⋯⋯1 $3/4$杯 罐頭斑豆（連汁，圖3）⋯$1 3/4$杯	$1^3/4$ tz. c/u: frijoles rojos y pintos enlatados, sin escurrir (Fig. 3)
$1/4$ c. finely diced dry parsley**	碎乾巴西利＊＊⋯⋯⋯⋯⋯$1/4$杯	$1/4$ tz. perejil seco finamente picado**
1 t. ea: ground cumin, finely diced dry oregano leaves**	小茴香粉⋯⋯⋯⋯⋯1小匙 碎乾俄力崗香料＊＊⋯⋯1小匙	1 c. c/u: comino molido, hojas de orégano secas**
1 T. chili powder	辣椒粉⋯⋯⋯⋯⋯⋯1大匙	1 C. chile en polvo
$1/2$ t. salt	鹽⋯⋯⋯⋯⋯⋯⋯$1/2$小匙	$1/2$ c. sal
$1/8$ t. pepper	胡椒⋯⋯⋯⋯⋯⋯$1/8$小匙	$1/8$ c. pimienta

3

$1/2$ c. shredded cheddar cheese	巧達起士絲⋯⋯⋯⋯⋯$1/2$杯	$1/2$ tz. queso Cheddar rallado
$1/4$ c. $1/4$" (0.5 cm) diced onions	洋蔥（切丁）⋯⋯⋯⋯$1/4$杯	$1/4$ tz. cebolla picada en cuadros de $1/4$" (0.5 cm)

1 Place **1** in deep pot, over medium heat. Break up meat while frying. Fry until meat is brown. Drain off grease.

2 Add **2** to pot, mix thoroughly with meat mixture, bring to boil, reduce heat, simmer uncovered 1 hour until thick but still moist. Stir occasionally. Serve and sprinkle on **3** for added flavor. For a variety of one-dish meals, try over cooked rice, tamales, or hot dogs.

★ Chili meat is coarse ground lean beef.

★★ 1 t. of finely diced dry herbs equals 1 T. loosely packed finely diced fresh herbs.

1 將 **1** 料放入無油無水的深鍋內，用中火炒開至肉變色倒出油。

2 隨入 **2** 料與肉拌勻燒開，降低火候不蓋鍋煮1小時至濃稠狀（中途需翻拌），上撒 **3** 料，可當主菜或澆在白飯、玉米粽或熱狗上食用。

★ 在超級市場有現成絞粗粒的粗牛絞瘦肉販賣稱Chili meat，本菜適用此種絞肉，若無可用一般牛絞肉取代。

★★ 乾香菜1小匙相當於新鮮切碎的香菜1大匙。

1 Ponga **1** en una olla honda a fuego moderado. Desbarate la carne mientras la cocina. Fría hasta que la carne esté dorada. Escurra la grasa.

2 Agregue **2** a la olla, mezcle completamente con la mezcla de carne, haga hervir, baje el fuego, cocine lentamente sin tapar por 1 hora hasta que esté espesa y aún húmeda. Revuelva ocasionalmente. Sirva y espolvoree **3** para aumentar el sabor. Como una variedad de comida de un solo platillo, pruébelo sobre arroz cocido, tamales o hot dogs.

★ Carne tipo chili es carne magra de res no picada finamente.

★★ 1 c. de hierbas secas finamente picadas equivale a 1 C. de hierbas frescas finamente picadas.

Vermicelli and Vegetables
Sopa Seca de Fideo

青豆煮麵

1

2

3

- Serves 4 -

**12 oz. (340g) coiled vermicelli*
(Fig. 1)**

1 | ¹/₂ c. ¹/₄" (0.5 cm) diced onions
¹/₂ garlic clove, minced

2 | 1 t. salt
¹/₄ t. pepper
2 c. canned ready-to-serve
  beef broth
2 c. water
1 c. tomato sauce

2 c. fresh or frozen peas

1 Heat 4 T. oil in large skillet over medium-high heat. Place vermicelli coils in skillet, fry on both sides until golden brown, push to one side. Add **1**, fry until onions are soft (Fig. 2).

2 Add **2**, bring to boil, reduce heat, cover and simmer 20 minutes.

3 Add peas and mix thoroughly until coils are separated. Cook 10 minutes until peas are tender, add water if needed. Rolls go well with this dish.

★ Vermicelli is a type of noodle also known as fideo. Spaghetti, angel hair, or linguine (Fig. 3), broken in half can be used if vermicelli is not available.

– 4人份 –

墨式麵條*（圖1）
　　‥‥‥‥‥9兩（340公克）

1 | 洋蔥（切丁）‥‥‥‥‥‥¹/₂杯
蒜（切碎）‥‥‥‥‥‥¹/₂瓣

2 | 鹽 ‥‥‥‥‥‥‥‥‥1小匙
胡椒 ‥‥‥‥‥‥‥¹/₄小匙
罐頭牛肉湯**（內含鹽）‥‥2杯
水 ‥‥‥‥‥‥‥‥‥2杯
番茄調味汁 ‥‥‥‥‥‥1杯

新鮮或冷凍青豆仁 ‥‥‥‥2杯

1 油4大匙燒熱，用中火將麵兩面煎呈金黃色，鏟於鍋邊，隨入 **1** 料炒至洋蔥軟（圖2）。

2 續入 **2** 料燒開，降低火候蓋鍋煮20分鐘。

3 再入青豆仁與麵一起拌開續煮10分鐘至青豆仁熟軟（如太乾可加入適量的水）。適合與麵包食用。

★ 墨式麵條是一種硬脆的細捲麵條，如無可用義大利麵條、義大利麵線或其他義大利麵條（圖3）取代。使用時折半使用。

**若使用一般自製高湯可酌加鹽³/₄小匙。

■ 此道菜的麵需在油內煎黃，故若用大平底鍋就可以一次全部放入煎，較易操作。

- 4 porciones -

12 oz. (340g) fideos enrollados* (Fig. 1)

1 | ¹/₂ tz. cebolla, picada en cuadros de ¹/₄" (0.5 cm)
¹/₂ diente de ajo, finamente picado

2 | 1 c. sal
¹/₄ c. pimienta
2 tz. c/u: caldo de res enlatado (listo para servir), agua
1 tz. salsa de tomate

2 tz. chícharos, frescos o congelados

1 Caliente 4 C. de aceite en un cacerola grande a fuego moderado. Ponga los rollos de fideos en el aceite, fría ambos lados hasta que estén dorados, muévalos a un lado. Agregue **1**, fría hasta que la cebolla esté blanda (Fig. 2).

2 Agregue **2**, haga hervir, baje el fuego, tape y cocine lentamente por 20 minutos.

3 Agregue los chícharos y mezcle completamente hasta que los rollos se separen. Cocine por 10 minutos hasta que los chícharos estén blandos, agregue agua si es necesario. Bolillos acompañan bien este platillo.

★ Vermicelli es un tipo de pasta llamada también fideo. Puede usar espagueti, cabellos de ángel o lengüini (Fig. 3), quebrados por la mitad, si no consigue vermicelli.

Meatball Soup
Sopa de Albóndigas

墨式肉丸湯

1

2

3

- 4人份 -

- 4 porciones -

1
- $^1/_2$ lb. (225g) ground beef
- 1 egg
- $^1/_2$ c. dry bread crumbs, plain
- $^1/_4$ t. salt
- $^1/_4$ t. ea: pepper, chili powder
- 1 T. finely diced dry parsley*
- $^1/_8$ c. raw long-grain rice

2
- 2 c. $^1/_2$" (1 cm) chopped tomatoes
- 2 c. ea: water, canned ready-to-use beef broth
- $^1/_2$ c. ea: $^1/_4$" (0.5 cm) diced onions, green bell peppers
- 1 T. finely diced dry parsley* (Fig.1)
- $^1/_2$ t. finely diced dry oregano leaves* (Fig.1)
- 1 t. salt
- $^1/_4$ t. pepper

3
- 1 $^1/_2$ c. $^1/_4$" (0.5 cm) sliced carrots
- 1 c. $^1/_2$" (1 cm) diced peeled potatoes

1
- 牛絞肉 ········6兩（225公克）
- 蛋 ·····················1個
- 麵包粉 ·················$^1/_2$杯
- 鹽 ·····················$^1/_2$小匙
- 胡椒 ···················$^1/_4$小匙
- 辣椒粉 ·················$^1/_4$小匙
- 碎乾巴西利* ···········1大匙
- 長米（再來米）········$^1/_8$杯

2
- 番茄（切小塊）·········2杯
- 水 ·····················2杯
- 罐頭牛肉湯**（內含鹽）·2杯
- 洋蔥（切丁）···········$^1/_2$杯
- 青椒（切丁）···········$^1/_2$杯
- 碎乾巴西利*（圖1）···1大匙
- 碎乾俄力崗香料*（圖1）
  ·······················$^1/_2$小匙
- 鹽 ·····················1小匙
- 胡椒 ···················$^1/_4$小匙

3
- 紅蘿蔔（切片）········1 $^1/_2$杯
- 馬鈴薯（切丁）··········1杯

1
- $^1/_2$ lb. (225g) carne molida de res
- 1 huevo
- $^1/_2$ tz. pan seco molido
- $^1/_2$ c. sal
- $^1/_4$ c. c/u: pimienta, chile en polvo
- 1 C. perejil seco, finamente picado*
- $^1/_8$ tz. arroz crudo de grano largo

2
- 2 tz. tomates cortados en $^1/_2$" (1 cm)
- 2 tz. c/u: agua, caldo de res enlatado listo para servir
- $^1/_2$ tz. c/u: cebolla, pimiento verde cortado en $^1/_4$" (0.5 cm)
- 1 C. perejil seco, finamente picado* (Fig. 1)
- $^1/_2$ c. hojas de orégano seco, finamente picado* (Fig. 1)
- 1 c. sal
- $^1/_4$ c. pimienta

3
- 1 $^1/_2$ tz. zanahoria en rebanadas de $^1/_4$" (0.5 cm)
- 1 tz. papas peladas en cubos de $^1/_2$" (1 cm)

---

1 Combine **1** , mix thoroughly. Form about 24 bite-size (1 rounded tablespoon of mixture) meatballs (Fig 2). Remove excess grease by putting meatballs on paper towels in flat dish and microwave 5 minutes; or pre-boil on stove.

2 Mix **2** in deep pot, add meatballs. Bring to boil, reduce heat, cover and simmer 30 minutes. Add **3** (Fig. 3) bring to boil and simmer 30 more minutes. Serve with warm bread, tortillas, or rolls.

* 1 t. of finely diced dry herbs equals 1 T. loosely packed finely diced fresh herbs.

1 將 **1** 料拌勻，揉成24個湯匙大小的肉丸（圖2）。如肉太肥可將紙巾鋪盤上，肉丸置紙巾上用微波爐加熱5分鐘去油。（買瘦肉即可免此一道手續）

2 將肉丸放入 **2** 料內燒開，去除白沫，改小火蓋鍋煮30分鐘，再加 **3** 料（圖3）燒開，改小火蓋鍋續煮30分鐘；與熱麵包或薄餅共食。

* 碎乾香菜1小匙相當於新鮮切碎的香菜1大匙。

** 若使用一般自製高湯可酌加鹽 $^3/_4$小匙。

1 Combine **1** , mezcle completamente. Forme como 24 albóndigas tamaño bocado (1 cucharada de la mezcla) (Fig. 2). Escurra el exceso de grasa poniendo las albóndigas sobre toallas de papel en un plato extendido en el horno de microondas por 5 minutos o calentándolas en una sartén en la estufa.

2 Mezcle **2** en una olla grande, agregue las albóndigas. Haga hervir, baje el fuego, tape y cocine lentamente por 30 minutos. Agregue **3** (Fig. 3) haga hervir y cocine lentamente por 30 minutos más. Sirva con pan caliente, tortillas o bolillos.

* 1 c. de hierbas secas equivale a 1 C. de hierbas frescas finamente picadas.

Chicken Kabob
Brochetas de Pollo

鶏肉串

1

2

3

- Serves 2 -

²/₃ lb. (300g) boneless chicken
(cut in 18 pieces, Fig. 1)

1
1 green pepper, cut in 18
pieces
12 sections green onion,
2" (5 cm) long

6 bamboo skewers (Fig. 2),
8" (20 cm) long

2
2 slices ginger
1 T. cornstarch
¹/₄ t. dashi (see p. 54, Fig. 1)
¹/₂ c. sugar
¹/₂ c. soy sauce
1 t. cooking wine
1 c. water

1 T. sesame seeds (fried)

1 Cook mixture **2** and stir gently until the sauce thickens.

2 Spear 3 pieces of meat on each skewer with pieces of **1** (Fig. 3) placed between each piece of meat as desired. Small tomatoes, onions or other vegetables may be added as desired.

3 Barbecue the kabobs over charcoal until cooked; turn constantly during the barbecue process. Remove; pour on cooked **2** then sprinkle with sesame seeds. Serve with rice if desired.

- 2人份 -

鷄肉（切18塊，圖1）
…………半斤（300公克）

1
青椒（切18塊）…………1個
蔥（5公分長）…………12段

竹籤（20公分長，圖2）…6枝

2
薑 …………………………2片
玉米粉 …………………1大匙
魚粉（見54頁，圖1）¹/₄小匙
糖 ………………………¹/₂杯
醬油 ……………………¹/₂杯
酒 ………………………1小匙
水 …………………………1杯

芝麻（炒熟）…………1大匙

1 將調勻的 **2** 料邊煮邊攪拌至燒開呈薄汁。

2 一枝竹籤串三塊鷄肉，在肉與肉之間隨意串上 **1** 料（圖3），也可加小番茄、洋蔥等（蔬菜無限制）。

3 將鷄肉串置炭火上邊翻面邊烤至肉熟取出，淋上煮好的 **2** 料及撒上芝麻，可與飯配食。

- 2 porciones -

²/₃ lb. (300g) pollo sin hueso
(cortado en 18 pedazos,
Fig. 1)

1
1 pimiento verde, cortado en
18 pedazos
12 pedazos de cebollín (parte
verde), 2" (5 cm) de largo

6 palillos de bambú (Fig. 2),
8" (20 cm) de largo

2
2 rebanadas de jengibre
1 C. maicena
¹/₄ c. dashi (vea p. 54, Fig. 1)
¹/₂ tz. azúcar
¹/₂ tz. salsa de soya
1 c. vino para cocinar
1 tz. agua

1 C. semillas de sésamo
(fritas)

1 Cocine la mezcla **2** y revuelva ligeramente hasta que la salsa se espese.

2 Inserte 3 pedazos de carne en cada palillo con pedazos de **1** (Fig. 3) colocados entre cada pedazo de carne al gusto. Si desea puede agregar tomates chicos, cebolla u otros vegetales.

3 Cocine las brochetas a la parrilla hasta que estén cocidas; voltee constantemente mientras las asa. Retire; cubra con **2** luego espolvoréeles las semillas de sésamo. Si desea sirva con arroz.

Shrimp & Salmon on Rice
Camarones y Salmón Sobre Arroz

鮭魚蝦飯

1

2

3

- Serves 2 -

8 jumbo shrimp

$^1/_3$ lb. (150g) smoked salmon (Fig. 1)

$^1/_2$ c. shredded onion

1 | 1 T. sesame seeds, fried
1 T. minced ginger

1 $^1/_2$ c. sliced Gherkin cucumbers

2 | $^1/_2$ t. salt
1 $^1/_2$ T. each: sugar, vinegar

$^3/_4$ c. round rice (Japanese)

3 | $^1/_4$ t. salt
$^3/_4$ t. sugar
$^3/_4$ T. vinegar

radish sprouts as desired

1 Shell shrimp, devein, and clean; place in boiling water until cooked. Slice salmon. Soak onions 30 minutes; remove (Fig. 2). Marinate cucumbers with **2** for 30 minutes; squeeze liquid out for later use.

2 Rinse rice; add no more than 3/4 c. water (less water as necessary to prevent cooked rice from sticking together) then cook until done to make sushi rice. Add **3** and stir while rice is hot (stir gently from bottom to avoid crushing rice). Let cool.

3 Add salmon, onions, **1** and cucumbers to rice; sprinkle on radish sprouts. Place cooked shrimp on top; serve with sashimi or hot soup.

■ Ready-made sushi vinegar (Fig. 3) may be purchased in oriental markets to substitute for **2**.

- 2人份 -

大蝦 ·················8條

燻鮭魚（圖1）···4兩(150公克)

洋蔥（切絲）···········$^1/_2$杯

1 | 芝麻（炒熟）········1大匙
薑末 ···············1大匙

小黃瓜（切片）·······1 $^1/_2$杯

2 | 鹽 ·············$^1/_2$小匙
糖 ···········1 $^1/_2$大匙
醋 ···········1 $^1/_2$大匙

蓬來米 ············$^3/_4$杯

3 | 鹽 ············$^1/_4$小匙
糖 ············$^3/_4$小匙
醋 ············$^3/_4$大匙

蘿蔔芽··············適量

1 蝦去殼、去腸洗淨，放入滾水內燙熟。燻鮭魚切片。洋蔥泡水30分鐘後撈出（圖2）。小黃瓜調 **2** 料醃30分鐘，擠乾水份備用。

2 米洗淨，加水$^2/_3$杯或略減煮成壽司飯（為免煮好的飯粒太粘，水量宜比平常煮飯略減）趁熱拌入 **3** 料（拌時輕輕由底部翻拌，以免米粒壓碎）待冷。

3 將魚、洋蔥、 **1** 料、小黃瓜全部拌入飯內，隨意撒上蘿蔔芽，上擺煮熟的蝦，可與生魚片或熱湯配食。

■ 市面上有賣現成的壽司醋（圖3），可用來取代 **2** 料。

- 2 porciones -

8 camarones grandes

$^1/_3$ lb. (150g) salmón ahumado (Fig. 1)

$^1/_2$ tz. cebolla cortada

1 | 1 C. semillas de sésamo, fritas
1 C. jengibre finamente picado

1 $^1/_2$ tz. pepinos gherkin en rebanadas

2 | $^1/_2$ c. sal
1 $^1/_2$ C. c/u: azúcar, vinagre

$^3/_4$ tz. arroz redondo (japonés)

3 | $^1/_4$ c. sal
$^3/_4$ c. azúcar
$^3/_4$ C. vinagre

brotes de rábano al gusto

1 Pele, desvene, y limpie los camarones; ponga en agua hirviendo hasta que se cocinen. Rebane el salmón. Remoje la cebolla por 30 minutos; retire (Fig. 2). Marine los pepinos con **2** por 30 minutos; escúrrale el líquido para usarlo después.

2 Enjuague el arroz; agregue no más de 3/4 tz. de agua (sólo agua necesaria para prevenir que se pegue el arroz cocido) luego cocine bien para hacer arroz sushi. Agregue **3** y revuelva mientras el arroz está caliente (revuelva cuidadosamente desde abajo para no machacar el arroz). Deje enfriar.

3 Agregue el salmón, cebolla, **1** y pepinos al arroz; espolvoréele los brotes de rábano. Coloque camarones cocidos encima; sirva con sashimi (pescado crudo) o sopa caliente.

■ Vinagre de sushi ya preparado (Fig. 3) se encuentra en mercados orientales y se puede substituir por **2**.

Home Style Hand Rolls (Temaki)
Rollos Caseros Hechos a Mano (Temaki)

家庭手捲

- Serves 2 -	- 2人份 -	- 2 porciones -

English:

1 6 medium shrimp
6 slices fresh sashimi
  (raw fish)
crab meat, egg, pork sung,
  canned meat, hot dog or
  other as desired

2 $^2/_3$ lb. (300g) of any
combination: sliced
avocado, cooked
asparagus, gherkin
cucumber (cut in strips),
radish sprouts, or lettuce
Pickled burdok or pickled
radish (takuwan) (Fig. 1),
cut in 14 strips

12 nori sheets*, 7" x 3 $^1/_2$"
  (18 cm x 9 cm)

1 $^1/_2$ c. sushi rice (see p. 45,
  step 2)

3 1 t. wasabi (see p. 56, Fig. 3)
1 t. soy sauce

2 t. mayonnaise

6 toothpicks

Chinese:

1 中蝦 ·················6隻
新鮮生魚 ·········6片
蟹肉、蛋、肉鬆、罐頭肉類、
熱狗等·············任選隨意

2 奶菓（切片）、蘆筍（燙熟）、
小黃瓜（切條）、蘿蔔芽或
生菜任選共半斤（300公克）
山根或漬黃蘿蔔（圖1）
 ·················切條共14條

紫菜*（18公分×9公分）12張

壽司飯（見45頁，作法2）
 ·····················1 $^1/_2$杯

3 山葵醬（見56頁，圖3）
 ·····················1小匙
醬油 ·················1小匙

美乃滋 ·················2小匙

牙籤 ·················6枝

Spanish:

1 6 camarones medianos
6 rebanadas de sashimi
  (pescado crudo) fresco
carne de cangrejo, huevo,
  cerdo sung, carne
  enlatada, hot dog o
  cualquier otra al gusto

2 $^2/_3$ lb. (300g) de cualquier
combinación: aguacate
rebanado, espárragos
cocidos, pepino gherkin
(cortado en tiras), brotes
de rábano, o lechuga.
burdock escabechado o
rábano escabechado
(takuwan) (Fig. 1),
cortado en 14 tiritas

12 hojas de nori*, 7" x 3 $^1/_2$"
  (18 cm x 9 cm)

1 $^1/_2$ tz arroz sushi (vea p. 45,
  paso 2)

3 1 c. wasabi (vea p. 56, Fig. 2)
1 c. salsa de soya

2 c. mayonesa

6 picadientes

English:

1 Shell shrimp, devein, and rinse. Skewer each shrimp with a toothpick to avoid shrinkage; place in boiling water until cooked. Remove toothpicks.

2 Arrange 1 1/2 T. sushi rice on each nori sheet then top with **1**, **2** (see dish photo and Figs. 2 & 3). Dab on a bit of mixture **3** or mayonnaise; roll nori into a horn shape. Serve.

★ Nori for hand-rolled sushi may be purchased in oriental markets; cut sheets in half if too large. To avoid softening by moisture, seal unused nori sheets in a bag. Before use, heat them in an oven a few seconds to increase crispiness.

■ Chili pepper or sesame seeds may be added in hand rolls if desired.

Chinese:

1 蝦去殼、去腸洗淨，串上牙籤（以免捲縮），放入滾水內燙熟後，取出牙籤備用。

2 紫菜上放1 $^1/_2$ 大匙的壽司飯，上置 **1** 、 **2** 料（參考大圖及小圖2、3），再抹少許調勻的 **3** 料或美乃滋，捲成喇叭或圓筒狀即可食用。

★ 市面上有賣專門做手捲用的紫菜，若是大張紫菜可剪半後使用。沒用完的紫菜需密封，以免潮濕變軟，使用前可放入烤箱內烤數秒鐘，增加其酥脆度。

■ 手捲內亦可加辣椒或芝麻。

Spanish:

1 Pele, desvene, y enjuague los camarones. Inserte cada camarón con un picadientes para prevenir que se encojan; coloque en agua hirviendo hasta que se cocinen. Quíteles los picadientes.

2 Coloque 1 1/2 C. de arroz sushi en cada hoja de nori, luego agregue **1** , **2** (vea la foto del platillo y Figs. 2 y 3). Unte un poco de la mezcla **3** ó mayonesa; enrolle el nori en forma de cuerno. Sirva.

★ Nori para enrollar sushi a mano se encuentra en mercados orientales; corte las hojas por la mitad si son muy grandes. Para prevenir que se remojen, guarde las hojas de nori no usadas en una bolsa cerrada. Antes de usarlas, caliéntelas en un horno por unos segundos para que estén más crujientes.

■ Se puede agregar chile o semillas de sésamo a los rollos si lo desea.

Japanese Style Rice
Arroz Estilo Japonés

親子飯

1

2

3

- Serves 2 -

1
¹/₃ lb. (150g) boneless chicken, cut in strips, (Fig. 1)
¹/₃ lb. (150g) shredded onion, (Fig. 2)

2
2 green onions, sliced diagonally, (Fig. 2)
3 eggs, beaten

3
¹/₂ t. dashi (see p. 54, Fig. 1)
1 T. sugar
1 T. mirin (see p. 54, Fig. 2) or rice wine
2 ¹/₂ T. soy sauce
³/₄ c. water

2 c. cooked rice

4
pickled ginger (Fig. 3) or pickled radish (see p. 46, Fig. 1) as desired

1 Bring **3** to boil. Add **1** , cover, and bring to boil; stir until chicken is cooked. Add **2** , cover, and cook until the eggs are half set (no need to stir); turn off heat immediately.

2 Put hot rice in 2 serving bowls and top with chicken mixture ; sprinkle
■ with chili powder. Serve with **4** .

Wood serving bowls with covers, may be used to enhance atmosphere and preserve warmness of rice.

- 2人份 -

1
鷄腿肉（切條，圖1）
⋯⋯⋯⋯4兩（150公克）
洋蔥（切絲，圖2）
⋯⋯⋯⋯4兩（150公克）

2
蔥（切斜片，圖2）⋯⋯⋯2支
蛋（打散）⋯⋯⋯⋯⋯3個

3
魚粉（見54頁，圖1） ¹/₂小匙
糖 ⋯⋯⋯⋯⋯⋯1大匙
味醂（見54頁，圖2）或米酒
⋯⋯⋯⋯⋯⋯1大匙
醬油 ⋯⋯⋯2¹/₂大匙
水 ⋯⋯⋯⋯³/₄杯

熱飯 ⋯⋯⋯⋯2碗

4
漬紅薑絲（圖3）或漬黃蘿蔔
（見46頁，圖1）⋯⋯隨意

1 將 **3** 料放入小鍋內燒開，隨入 **1** 料蓋鍋，燒開後略攪，見鷄肉熟放入 **2** 料再蓋鍋待蛋呈半熟狀（不需攪拌）即熄火。

2 熱飯分裝於碗內，上置煮好的料，隨意撒辣椒粉並與 **4** 料配食。

■ 若用有蓋的木碗裝飯，可增加情調並有保溫作用。

- 2 porciones -

1
¹/₃ lb. (150g) pollo sin hueso, cortado en tiras (Fig. 1)
¹/₃ lb. (150g) cebolla rallada (Fig. 2)

2
2 cebollines, rebanados diagonalmente (Fig. 2)
3 huevos, batidos

3
¹/₂ c. dashi (vea p. 54, Fig. 1)
1 C. azúcar
1 C. mirin (vea p. 54, Fig. 2) o vino de arroz
2 ¹/₂ C. salsa de soya
³/₄ tz. agua

2 tz. arroz cocido

4
jengibre escabechado (Fig. 3) o rábano escabechado (vea p. 46, Fig. 1) al gusto

1 Haga hervir **3** . Agregue **1** , tape, y haga hervir; revuelva hasta que el pollo esté cocido. Agregue **2** , tape, y cocine hasta que los huevos estén medio cocidos (no necesita revolver); apague el fuego de inmediato.

2 Divida el arroz caliente en 2 tazones a servir y cubra con la mezcla de pollo; espolvoree con
■ chile en polvo. Sirva con **4** .

Puede usar tazones de madera con tapadera para armonizar el ambiente y mantener caliente el arroz.

Seafood Combination
Combinación de Mariscos

海鮮燒

1

2

3

- Serves 2 -

1. Total of ¹/₂ lb. (225g) (cut in pieces): fresh scallops, white fish filet
   ¹/₂ T. masago

   4 T. mayonnaise

2. ¹/₂ c. mushrooms or canned straw mushrooms
   1 c. minced onion

   2 slices cheese (Fig. 1)

1 Mix **1** (Fig. 2) with mayonnaise; add **2** . Place in 2 abalone shells or other containers (Fig. 3).

2 Bake 7 minutes in a small oven. Remove; put cheese on top then bake for 1 more minute. Serve with rice or noodles.

- 2人份 -

1. 鮮干貝、白色魚肉
   ⋯⋯切塊共6兩（225公克）
   魚子 ⋯⋯⋯⋯⋯⋯⋯¹/₂大匙

   美乃滋 ⋯⋯⋯⋯⋯⋯4大匙

2. 毛菇或罐頭草菇（切片）¹/₂杯
   洋蔥（切碎）⋯⋯⋯⋯⋯1杯

   起士（圖1）⋯⋯⋯⋯⋯2片

1 將 **1** 料（圖2）拌入美乃滋，再拌 **2** 料，分別裝入2個鮑魚殼或其他容器內（圖3）。

2 將準備好的料連同容器一齊放入小烤箱內（以烤土司麵包的方式）烤7分鐘取出，上置起士再烤約1分鐘。可與飯或麵配食。

- 2 porciones -

1. ¹/₂ lb. (225g) en total: escalopes frescos, filete de pescado blanco (cortado en pedazos)
   ¹/₂ C. masago (huevos de pescado)

   4 C. mayonesa

2. ¹/₂ tz. hongos u hongos enlatados (straw mushrooms)
   1 tz. cebolla picada

   2 tajadas de queso (Fig. 1)

1 Mezcle **1** (Fig. 2) con mayonesa; agregue **2** . Acomode en 2 conchas de abalone u otro recipiente (Fig. 3).

2 Cocine por 7 minutos en un horno pequeño. Retire; agregue el queso arriba y hornee 1 minuto más. Sirva con arroz o fideos.

Udon in Broth
Caldo de Fideos Udon

鍋焼烏龍麺

1

2

3

1 1 lb. (450g) cooked udon
   noodles* (see p. 58,
   Fig. 1), 2 pkgs
   ¹/₃ lb. (150g) nappa cabbage
   or vegetable of choice,
   cut in pieces

2 6 slices fish cake
   (kamaboko) (Fig. 1)
   ¹/₃ lb. (150g) boneless
   chicken, sliced, (Fig. 2)
   4 shrimp
   4 Chinese black mushrooms
   (Fig. 3), presoftened

3 2 eggs
   2 green onions, cut 2" (5 cm)
   long

4 1 ¹/₂ t. salt
   2 t. dashi (see p. 54, Fig. 1)
   2 t. mirin (see p. 54, Fig. 2)
   or cooking wine
   2 t. soy sauce

1 This dish is traditionally cooked one serving at a time, and then served in the pot in which it was cooked.
Bring 2 1/2 c. water with half of **4** to boil. Add half of **1** and boil again; (stir to separate udon noodles). Add half of **2**, cover, and bring to another boil. Add half of **3** when chicken is done; cook until egg is half set. Repeat procedures to complete the other serving. Chili powder may be added as desired.

* Ready-made cooked udon noodles with a seasoning packet may be purchased in oriental markets. The seasoning may be used for **4**. If dried noodles are used, cook before placing in soup.

■ Clams, squid or other seafood of choice may be added to soup. This dish is ideal for those who favor hot food.

1 熟烏龍麵*（見58頁，圖1）
   2包 ‥‥‥‥12兩（450公克）
   白菜或其他蔬菜（切塊）
   ‥‥‥‥‥‥4兩（150公克）

2 魚板（圖1）‥‥‥‥‥‥6片
   雞肉（切片，圖2）
   ‥‥‥‥‥‥4兩（150公克）
   蝦 ‥‥‥‥‥‥‥‥‥4條
   香菇（圖3，泡軟）‥‥‥‥4個

3 蛋 ‥‥‥‥‥‥‥‥‥2個
   蔥（切5公分長）‥‥‥‥‥2支

4 鹽 ‥‥‥‥‥‥‥1 ¹/₂小匙
   魚粉（見54頁，圖1）‥2小匙
   味醂（見54頁，圖2）或米酒
   ‥‥‥‥‥‥‥‥‥2小匙
   醬油 ‥‥‥‥‥‥‥‥2小匙

1 本麵宜一人份一鍋燒煮，食用時連鍋上桌。
將水2¹/₂杯加¹/₂的 **4** 料燒開，先入¹/₂的 **1** 料再燒開（烏龍麵須用筷子攪散），隨入¹/₂的 **2** 料蓋鍋燒開，見雞肉熟，再加¹/₂的 **3** 料煮至蛋呈半熟狀即可；另一份可依法做。食時可隨意加辣椒粉。

* 市面上有賣熟烏龍麵，內附的調味包，可用來取代 **4** 料。若用乾烏龍麵需另燒開水將麵煮熟再放入湯內。

■ 湯內可隨喜好加蛤蜊、魷魚等，對喜愛熱食者，是為理想便餐。

1 1 lb. (450g) 2 paquetes,
   fideos udon cocidos*
   (vea p. 58, Fig. 1)
   ¹/₃ lb. (150g) repollo napa o
   vegetal de su gusto,
   cortado en pedazos

2 6 rebanadas de pan de
   pescado (kamabobo)
   (Fig. 1)
   ¹/₃ lb (150g) pollo deshuesado
   en rebanadas (Fig. 2)
   4 camarones
   4 hongos negros chinos, ya
   ablandados (Fig. 3)

3 2 huevos
   2 cebollines verdes, cortados a
   lo largo 2" (5 cm)

4 1 ¹/₂ c. sal
   2 c. dashi (vea p. 54, Fig. 1)
   2 c. mirin (vea p. 54, Fig. 2) o
   vino para cocinar
   2 c. salsa de soya

1 Ponga a hervir 2 1/2 tz. de agua con la mitad de **4**. Agregue la mitad de **1** y hierva otra vez; (revuelva para separar los fideos udon). Agregue la mitad de **2**, tape y vuelva a hervir. Agregue la mitad de **3** cuando el pollo esté cocido; cocine hasta que el huevo esté medio cuajado. Repita el procedimiento para completar la otra porción. Si lo desea, puede agregar chile en polvo.

* Fideos udon ya cocidos, con un paquetito de condimentos se pueden adquirir en los mercados orientales. El condimento se puede usar para **4**. Si usa fideos secos, cocínelos antes de agregarlos a la sopa.

■ A esta sopa se le puede agregar almejas, calamares u otros mariscos de su agrado. Este es un platillo ideal para quienes prefieren la comida picante.

Beef Sukiyaki
Sukiyaki de Res

牛肉壽喜燒

1

2

3

- Serves 2 -

$^2/_3$ lb. (300g) beef slices

1 T. butter

2 green onions, cut 2" (5 cm) long

1
- 1 t. dashi (Fig. 1)
- 2 T. sugar
- $^1/_4$ c. mirin (Fig. 2) or rice wine
- $^1/_4$ c. soy sauce
- $^1/_2$ c. water

2
- 2 tofu ($^1/_2$ lb., 225g), cut in pieces
- 2 Chinese black mushrooms, (presoftened)
- 1 shredded onion
- 1 c. shredded shirataki (Fig. 3)

3
- Total of 1 lb. (450g): nappa cabbage (cut in pieces), spinach, garland chrysanthemum or golden mushrooms

2 eggs

- 2人份 -

牛肉片 ……半斤（300公克）

奶油 ………………………1大匙

蔥（切5公分長）…………2支

1
- 魚粉（圖1）…………1小匙
- 糖 ………………………2大匙
- 味醂（圖2）或米酒 ……$^1/_4$杯
- 醬油 …………………………$^1/_4$杯
- 水 ……………………………$^1/_2$杯

2
- 豆腐（切塊） 2塊（225公克）
- 香菇（泡軟）…………………2朵
- 洋蔥（切絲）…………………1個
- 蒟蒻絲（圖3）………………1杯

3
- 大白菜（切塊）、菠菜或唐好菜、金針菇共12兩（450公克）

蛋 ……………………………2個

- 2 porciones -

$^2/_3$ lb. (300g) carne de res en rebanadas

1 C. mantequilla

2 cebollines verdes, cortados a lo largo 2" (5 cm)

1
- 1 c. dashi (Fig. 1)
- 2 C. azúcar
- $^1/_4$ tz. mirin (Fig. 2) o vino de arroz
- $^1/_4$ tz. salsa de soya
- $^1/_2$ tz. agua

2
- 2 paquetes de tofu ($^1/_2$ lb., 225g) cortado en pedazos
- 2 hongos negros chinos (ablandados previamente)
- 1 cebolla rallada
- 1 tz. shirataki picada (Fig. 3)

3
- 1 lb. (450g) en total: repollo napa (cortado en pedazos), espinaca, guirnalda de crisantemos u hongos dorados

2 huevos

---

1 Heat 1 T. butter in a pot, placed on a table-top stove, hibachi, or electric hot plate. Stir-fry onions briefly; add in beef slices one by one. Pour 1/2 c. of mixture **1** and stir well; move to the side of the pot.

2 Add **2**; pour in the remaining **1** and bring to boil. Move meat from the side of the pot to top of **2** when meat changes color. Add **3** during cooking according to individual preference.

3 Beat eggs and place in separate bowls; dip cooked ingredients in egg and serve with rice.

---

1 鍋置餐桌上，奶油1大匙燒熱，入蔥略炒，把牛肉一片一片放入，淋上$^1/_2$杯調勻的 **1** 料翻拌，推至一邊。

2 將 **2** 料也放入鍋內，淋入剩餘的 **1** 料燒開，見鍋邊的肉變色後將肉置 **2** 料上，邊煮邊將 **3** 料依喜好放入煮熟。

3 蛋分置小碗內打散，將煮好的材料沾蛋液與飯配食。

---

1 Caliente 1 C. mantequilla en una olla, ponga en una cocinilla para la mesa, hibachi o plato eléctrico caliente. Fría-revolviendo las cebollas brevemente; agregue las rebanadas de carne una por una. Vacíele 1/2 tz. de la mezcla **1** y revuelva bien; deje en la orilla de la olla.

2 Agregue **2**; vacíe el resto de **1** y ponga a hervir. Mueva la carne de la orilla a encima de **2** cuando la carne cambie de color. Agregue **3** mientras cocine, de acuerdo a su gusto personal.

3 Bata los huevos y póngalos en los dos tazones, unte los ingredientes cocidos en el huevo y sirva con arroz.

Cold Seafood Noodles
Fideos Fríos con Mariscos

三色涼麵

1

2

3

- Serves 2 -	- 2人份 -	- 2 porciones -

¹/₃ lb. (150g) dried noodles (Fig. 1)

6 shrimp

2 strips crab meat (Fig. 2)

2 eggs

1. Total of ¹/₃ lb. (150g); shredded: gherkin cucumbers, carrot

2. 1 t. dashi (see p. 54, Fig. 1)
   1 t. mirin (see p. 54, Fig. 2) or rice wine
   3 T. soy sauce
   ¹/₂ c. water

3. 2 T. chopped green onion
   4 T. nori, shredded
   1 t. wasabi paste* (Japanese horseradish) (Fig. 3)

乾麵（圖1）…4兩（150公克）

蝦 …………………………6條

蟹肉（圖2）……………2條

蛋 …………………………2個

1. 黃瓜、紅蘿蔔
   ……切絲共4兩（150公克）

2. 魚粉（見54頁，圖1）…1小匙
   味醂（見54頁，圖2）或米酒
   …………………………1小匙
   醬油 ……………………3大匙
   水 ……………………¹/₂杯

3. 蔥花 ……………………2大匙
   紫菜絲 …………………4大匙
   山葵醬*（圖3）………1小匙

¹/₃ lb. (150g) fideos secos (Fig. 1)

6 camarones

2 tiras de carne de cangrejo (Fig. 2)

2 huevos

1. ¹/₃ lb. (150g) en total: pepinos gherkin, zanahoria, rallados

2. 1 c. dashi (vea p. 54, Fig. 1)
   1 c. mirin (vea p. 54, Fig. 2) o vino de arroz
   3 C. salsa de soya
   ¹/₂ tz. agua

3. 2 C. cebollín verde picado
   4 C. nori (alga marina) cortada
   1 c. pasta de wasabi* (rábano picante japonés) (Fig. 3)

---

1 Select one or several colors, but use the same noodle thickness. Cook noodles according to the instructions on the package. Remove, plunge in cold water, then drain. Remove shrimp shells, devein, and rinse; put in boiling water until cooked then remove. Tear crab meat into shreds.

2 Heat wok; add 1 t. oil. Spread the oil evenly on surface of the wok with a paper towel. Beat eggs, fry into a thin pancake, and shred.

3 Mix **2** well; when serving, add **3** to make dipping sauce.

4 Put noodles in 2 serving bowls; top with shrimp, egg shreds, crab meat and **1**. To serve, dip the noodles in dipping sauce, or mix desired amount of sauce with the noodles.

★ If using wasabi powder, mix 1 t. water with the powder, cover tightly, then let stand for 10 minutes.

---

1 將一種或數種顏色，同樣粗細的麵依包裝指示將麵煮熟，漂過涼水後瀝乾。蝦去殼、去腸洗淨，放入滾水內燙熟。蟹肉撕成絲狀。

2 鍋燒熱，入油1小匙用紙巾擦勻鍋面（使鍋面有一層油）將蛋打散煎成蛋皮後切絲備用。

3 **2** 料調勻，食時拌入 **3** 料即成沾料。

4 將麵分裝於碗內，上擺蝦、蛋皮絲、蟹肉及 **1** 料，沾沾料或將適量的沾料淋入麵內食用。

★ 若是山葵粉，需先用水1小匙攪拌蓋緊，放置10分鐘後使用。

■ 此道菜最適合於炎夏食用。

---

1 Seleccione uno o varios colores, pero use fideos del mismo grosor. Cocine los fideos siguiendo las instrucciones del paquete. Retire, sumerja en agua fría, luego cuele. Pele los camarones, desvénelos y enjuague; cocínelos en agua hirviendo hasta que estén cocidos, luego sáquelos. Corte la carne de cangrejo en hebras.

2 Caliente la sartén wok; agregue 1 c. de aceite. Con toalla de papel unte con aceite la superficie de la sartén en forma pareja. Bata los huevos, fría, forme un panqueque delgado y desbarátelo.

3 Mezcle bien **2**; al servir, agregue **3** para formar una salsa para untar.

4 Ponga los fideos en dos tazones; acomode encima los camarones, las hebras de huevo, la carne de cangrejo y **1**. Al servir, unte los fideos en la salsa para untar, o mezcle con los fideos la cantidad de salsa que guste.

★ Si usa polvo de wasabi, mezcle 1 c. de agua con el polvo, tape completamente, deje reposar por 10 minutos.

Fried Udon Noodles
Fideos Udon Fritos

炒烏龍麵

1

2

3

- Serves 2 -

2 packages (1 lb., 450g)
    precooked udon noodles
    (Fig. 1)

$^1/_2$ lb. (225g) boneless chicken
    legs, shredded

2 green onions

2 T. soy sauce

1 | Total of $^2/_3$ lb. (300g),
    shredded (Fig. 2): onions,
    cabbage, carrots

2 | $^1/_4$ t. each: salt, pepper
    $^1/_2$ t. dashi (see p. 54, Fig. 1)
    $^1/_2$ c. water

1 c. bean sprouts (optional)

1 Immerse the precooked udon noodles in boiling water briefly, stir to separate the noodles, then remove. Diagonally cut green onions; separate green part and white part (Fig. 3).

2 Heat 2 T. oil. Stir-fry white onion pieces until fragrant; add meat and stir-fry until separated and cooked. Add soy sauce, and **1** ; stir-fry briefly. Add mixture **2** , cover, and bring to boil. Add noodles and stir-fry until the sauce is evaporated. Add bean sprouts and green onion pieces; stir briefly. Serve.

－ 2人份 －

熟烏龍麵（圖1）2包
　　　……… 12兩（450公克）

鷄腿肉（切絲）6兩（225公克）

蔥 ………………………… 2支

醬油 ………………… 2大匙

1 | 洋蔥、高麗菜、紅蘿蔔（切絲，圖2）　共半斤（300公克）

2 | 鹽 …………………… $^1/_4$小匙
胡椒 ………………… $^1/_4$小匙
魚粉（見54頁，圖1）$^1/_2$小匙
水 ……………………… $^1/_2$杯

豆芽菜（無亦可）……… 1杯

1 麵在滾水內川燙，用筷子攪散撈出；蔥斜切分蔥白、蔥綠（圖3）。

2 油2大匙燒熱，炒香蔥白，入肉炒開至熟，拌入醬油，加 **1** 料略炒並加調勻的 **2** 料蓋鍋燒開，再入麵炒至汁收乾，加豆芽菜及蔥綠略拌即成。

■ 烏龍麵有生、乾及煮熟的三種可任選使用。

- 2 porciones -

2 paquetes (1 lb., 450g)
    fideos udon precocidos
    (Fig. 1)

$^1/_2$ lb. (225g) piernas de pollo,
    sin hueso, desmenuzadas

2 cebollines verdes

2 C. salsa de soya

1 | $^2/_3$ lb. (300g) en total: cebolla,
    repollo, zanahoria
    picados (Fig. 2)

2 | $^1/_4$ c. c/u: sal, pimienta
    $^1/_2$ c. dashi (vea p. 54, Fig. 1)
    $^1/_2$ tz. agua

1 tz. brotes de frijol
    (opcional)

1 Sumerja brevemente los fideos udon precocidos en agua hirviendo, revuelva para separar los fideos, luego retire. Corte los cebollines diagonalmente; separe la parte blanca de la verde (Fig. 3).

2 Caliente 2 C. de aceite. Fría-revolviendo la parte blanca del cebollín hasta que esté aromático; agregue la carne y fría-revolviendo hasta que la carne esté separada y cocida. Agregue la salsa de soya y **1** ; fría-revolviendo brevemente. Agregue la mezcla **2** , tape, y haga hervir. Agregue los fideos y fría-revolviendo hasta que la salsa se evapore. Agregue los brotes de frijol y el cebollín; revuelva brevemente. Sirva.

Fettuccine alla Zorio (Fettuccine Zorio)
Fettuccine Zorio

義大利起士麵

2

3

- Serves 4 -

6 bacon strips

1
½ lb. (225g) fresh
mushrooms, sliced
¼ c. ¼" (0.5 cm) diced onions
1 garlic clove, minced
(optional)

12 oz. (340g) fettuccine
noodles (Fig. 1)

2
⅓ c. soft butter
½ c. sour cream
1 c. whipping cream or half
and half cream
½ c. grated Parmesan cheese
1 c. fresh or frozen peas

1 Fry bacon until crisp, drain on
paper towels, cut into small
pieces and set aside (Fig. 2).
Heat 2 T. bacon grease in skillet,
add ❶ (Fig. 3) and saute over
medium heat until soft. Drain
liquid, set aside.

2 Put 6 c. water and 1 t. oil in deep
pot, bring to boil, add fettuccine
noodles. Cook 9 minutes until
tender, stirring occasionally.
Drain noodles and rinse with
warm water, put back in pot.

3 Add ❶ , ❷ , and bacon to pot, mix,
cook over medium heat for 5
minutes until peas are tender,
stirring occasionally. Serve
immediately. Salad, bread and
red wine go well with this meal.

－ 4人份 －

培根 ·····················6條

1
新鮮洋菇（切片）
·············6兩（225公克）
洋蔥（切丁）···············¼杯
蒜（切碎、無亦可）········1瓣

義大利寬麵條（圖1）
·············9兩（340公克）

2
奶油 ·····················⅓杯
酸奶油 ····················½杯
鮮奶油或半奶精 ··········1杯
巴馬起士（切碎）·········½杯
新鮮或冷凍青豆仁 ········1杯

1 將培根煎炸至酥脆，置於紙巾
上吸油，切小塊（圖2）備用。
留油2大匙用中火將 ❶ 料（圖
3）炒軟，倒出水份備用。

2 將水6杯與油1小匙放入深鍋內
燒開，隨入麵煮9分鐘至熟
（中途需攪拌）撈出麵，用溫水
略沖撈出。

3 將麵、 ❷ 料及培根放入炒好的
❶ 料鍋內，用中火翻拌煮約5
分鐘至青豆仁軟，趁熱食用。
適合與沙拉、麵包、紅酒共
食。

- 4 porciones -

6 rebanadas de tocino

1
½ lb. (225g) hongos frescos,
rebanados
¼ tz. cebolla picada en
cubitos de ¼" (0.5 cm)
1 diente de ajo, finamente
picado (opcional)

12 oz. (340g) fideos
fettuccine (Fig. 1)

2
⅓ tz. mantequilla blanda
½ tz. crema agria
1 tz. crema batida o crema de
leche
½ tz. queso Parmesano
rallado
1 tz. chícharos frescos o
congelados

1 Fría el tocino hasta que esté
crujiente, escurra en toallas de
papel, corte en pedazos chicos y
deje aparte (Fig. 2). Caliente 2 C.
de la grasa del tocino en una
cacerola, agregue ❶ (Fig. 3) y
sofría a fuego moderado hasta que
se ablande. Escurra el líquido, deje
aparte.

2 Ponga 6 tz. de agua y 1 C. de
aceite en una olla honda, haga
hervir, agregue los fideos. Cocine
por 9 minutos hasta que se
ablanden, revolviendo ocasionalmente. Escurra los fideos y
enjuague con agua tibia, devuél-
valos a la olla.

3 Agregue ❶ , ❷ , y el tocino a la
olla, mezcle, cocine a fuego
moderado por 5 minutos hasta
que los chícharos estén tiernos,
revolviendo ocasionalmente. Sirva
de inmediato. Este platillo se
complementa con ensalada, pan, y
vino tinto.

Capellini ai Frutti di Mare (Angel Hair Pasta & Seafood)

Cabello de Ángel y Mariscos

義大利海鮮麵線

1

2

3

- Serves 2 -

1/4 lb. (115g) medium-size raw shelled shrimp (Fig. 1)
1/4 lb. (115g) bay scallops (Fig. 1)

1
1/2 c. 1/2" (1 cm) diced onions
1 garlic clove, minced (optional)

2
2 c. 3/4" (2 cm) chopped ripe tomatoes
1 t. salt
1/8 t. pepper
1/2 t. sugar
2 T. finely diced dry parsley*

8 oz. (225g) angel hair pasta (Fig. 2)

---

1. Devein shrimp (Fig. 3), rinse and pat dry with paper towels. Heat 1 T. butter in skillet over high heat. Saute shrimp and scallops until cooked. Set aside and keep warm.

2. Prepare sauce: Heat 2 T. olive oil in pot over medium heat. Add **1** and saute until soft, add **2**, bring to boil, lower heat and simmer uncovered for 15 minutes, stirring occasionally.

3. Put 6 c. water and 1 t. oil in separate pot and bring to boil. Add pasta, cook 5 minutes until tender. Drain and rinse with warm water. Lightly toss with 1 T. olive oil (optional).

4. Place pasta servings on plates, spoon on sauce and top with seafood. Serve with bread sticks or rolls and white wine.

* 1 t. of finely diced dry herbs equals 1 T. of loosely packed finely diced fresh herbs.

- 2人份 -

去殼中蝦（圖1）
⋯⋯⋯⋯⋯3兩（115公克）

干貝（圖1）⋯3兩（115公克）

1
洋蔥（切丁）⋯⋯⋯⋯⋯1/2杯
蒜（切碎、無亦可）⋯⋯⋯1瓣

2
熟番茄（切小塊）⋯⋯⋯⋯2杯
鹽 ⋯⋯⋯⋯⋯⋯⋯⋯1小匙
胡椒 ⋯⋯⋯⋯⋯⋯⋯1/8小匙
糖 ⋯⋯⋯⋯⋯⋯⋯⋯1/2小匙
碎乾巴西利* ⋯⋯⋯⋯2大匙

義大利麵線（圖2）
⋯⋯⋯⋯⋯6兩（225公克）

---

1. 蝦去腸泥（圖3）洗淨，擦乾水份。奶油1大匙燒熱，隨入蝦、干貝煮約8分鐘至熟，保溫備用。

2. 橄欖油2大匙燒熱，隨入 **1** 料中火炒至洋蔥軟，續入 **2** 料燒開，略降火候不蓋鍋煮15分鐘（中途需攪拌）即成番茄麵醬。

3. 水6杯加油1小匙燒開，放入麵線煮約5分鐘撈出，用溫水略沖撈出（可隨意拌入橄欖油1大匙）。

4. 將煮好的麵線分置於盤內，澆上番茄麵醬，上置煮好的海鮮，並與麵包、白酒共食。

★ 碎乾巴西利1小匙相當於新鮮切碎的巴西利1大匙。

- 2 porciones -

1/4 lb. (115g) camarones medianos, crudos, pelados (Fig. 1)
1/4 lb. (115g) escalopes (Fig. 1)

1
1/2 tz. cebolla picada en cubitos de 1/2" (1 cm)
1 diente de ajo, finamente picado (opcional)

2
2 tz. tomates maduros picados en pedazos de 3/4" (2 cm)
1 c. sal
1/8 c. pimienta
1/2 c. azúcar
2 C. perejil seco finamente picado*

8 oz. (225g) fideo cabello de ángel (Fig. 2)

---

1. Desvene los camarones (Fig. 3), enjuague y seque ligeramente con toallas de papel. Caliente 1 C. de mantequilla en una sartén a fuego alto. Sofría los camarones y escalopes hasta que estén cocidos. Deje aparte y mantenga caliente.

2. Prepare la salsa: Caliente 2 C. de aceite de oliva en una cacerola a fuego moderado. Agregue **1** y sofría hasta que esté blando, agregue **2**, haga hervir, baje el fuego y cocine lentamente sin tapar por 15 minutos, revolviendo ocasionalmente.

3. Ponga 6 tz. de agua y 1 c. de aceite en una olla y haga hervir. Agregue los fideos, cocine por 5 minutos hasta que se ablanden. Escurra y enjuague con agua tibia. Mezcle ligeramente con 1 C. de aceite de oliva (opcional).

4. Divida los fideos en los platos a servir, vacíeles la salsa a cucharadas y cubra con los mariscos. Sirva con palitos de pan o bolillos y vino blanco.

★ 1 c. de hierbas secas finamente picadas equivale a 1 C. de hierbas frescas finamente picadas.

Spaghetti con Polpette (Spaghetti with Meatballs)
Espagueti con Albóndigas

義大利肉丸麵

1

2

3

- Serves 4 -

Meatballs:
¹/₄ lb. (225g) ground beef

1. ¼ c. finely diced onions
1 T. finely diced dry parsley*
½ t. salt, ¼ t. pepper
¼ c. dry bread crumbs, plain
1 egg, beaten

Sauce:
1 c. finely diced onions

2. 4 ½ lbs. (2025g) ripe tomatoes, (or Italian plum tomatoes) peeled, cored, and chopped
2 t. ea: finely diced dry basil and oregano leaves*
¾ t. salt, ½ t. pepper
¾ c. dry red wine

Spaghetti:
1 lb. (450g) spaghetti (Fig. 1)
½ c. grated Parmesan cheese, optional

1. Break up beef in bowl, add 1 , mix well. Form mixture into 1 1/2" (4 cm) balls (Fig. 2). Heat 2 T. olive oil in skillet over medium heat, add meatballs and brown on all sides (Fig. 3). Remove, drain on paper towels, set aside.

2. Prepare sauce by heating 4 T. olive oil in deep pot over medium heat. Add onions and saute until soft. Add 2 , finely mash tomatoes, boil 3 minutes stirring occasionally, reduce heat, and simmer uncovered for 30 minutes, stir occasionally until sauce thickens. Add meatballs and simmer 10 minutes.

3. Bring 10 c. water and 1 t. oil in pot to a boil. Add spaghetti, cook 10 minutes until tender, stir occasionally. Drain in colander, rinse with warm water. To serve, pour sauce and meatballs over spaghetti. Sprinkle on Parmesan cheese if desired. Salad, bread and wine go well with this dish.

* 1 t. of finely diced dry herbs equals 1 T. of loosely packed finely diced fresh herbs.

- 4人份 -

肉丸：
牛絞肉 ………6兩（225公克）

1. 洋蔥（切碎）…………………¹/₄杯
碎乾巴西利* …………1大匙
鹽…¹/₂小匙，胡椒 …¹/₄小匙
麵包粉…¹/₄杯，蛋(打散)…1個

義大利麵醬：
洋蔥（切粹）…………………1杯

2. 熟番茄（一般圓型或義大利長番茄去皮、去籽、切丁）
………3斤6兩（2025公克）
碎乾九層塔* ………2小匙
碎乾俄力崗香料* ……2小匙
鹽…³/₄小匙，胡椒……¹/₂小匙
紅酒………………………³/₄杯

義大利麵：
乾義大利麵（圖1）
…………12兩（450公克）
巴馬起士（切碎，無亦可）¹/₂杯

1. 將牛絞肉與 1 料拌勻，揉成直徑3.8公分的肉丸（圖2）。橄欖油2大匙燒熱，用中火將肉丸表面煎成金黃色（圖3）撈出，置於紙巾上吸乾油份備用。

2. 橄欖油4大匙燒熱，用中火將洋蔥炒軟，隨入 2 料將番茄壓爛燒開，略攪拌煮約3分鐘後略降火候不蓋鍋續煮30分鐘（中途需攪拌）至汁呈濃稠狀即成義大利麵醬，再加肉丸煮10分鐘即可。

3. 水10杯加油1小匙燒開，放入乾義大利麵煮10分鐘至熟（中途需攪拌）撈出，用溫水略沖，分置盤內，澆上義大利麵醬及肉丸，可隨意撒上巴馬起士。適合與沙拉、麵包及酒一齊食用。

★ 碎乾香菜1小匙相當於新鮮切碎的香菜1大匙。

- 4 porciones -

Albóndigas:
¹/₄ lb. (225g) carne molida de res

1. ¼ tz. cebolla finamente picada
1 C. perejil seco finamente picado*
½ c. sal, ¼ c. pimienta
¼ tz. pan seco molido
1 huevo, batido

Salsa:
1 tz. cebolla finamente picada

2. 4 ½ lbs. (2025g) tomates maduros, (o tomates Roma) pelados, sin semillas y picados
2 c. c/u: hojas de albahaca, hojas de orégano, secas finamente picadas*
¾ c. sal, ½ c. pimienta
¾ tz. vino tinto seco

Espagueti:
1 lb. (450g) espagueti (Fig. 1)
½ tz. queso Parmesano rallado, opcional

1. Desbarate la carne en un tazón, agregue 1 , mezcle bien. Forme la mezcla en albóndigas de 1 1/2" (4 cm) (Fig. 2). Caliente 2 C. de aceite de oliva en una sartén a fuego moderado, agregue las albóndigas y dore completamente (Fig. 3). Retire, escurra sobre toallas de papel, deje aparte.

2. Prepare la salsa calentando 4 C. de aceite de oliva en una sartén honda a fuego moderado. Agregue la cebolla y sofría hasta que se ablande. Agregue 2 , muela los tomates finamente, haga hervir por 3 minutos revolviendo ocasionalmente, baje el fuego, y cocine lentamente sin tapar por 30 minutos, revuelva ocasionalmente hasta que la salsa espese. Agregue las albóndigas y cocine lentamente por 10 minutos.

3. En una olla haga hervir 10 tz. de agua y 1 c. de aceite. Agregue el espagueti, cocine por 10 minutos hasta que se ablande, revuelva ocasionalmente. Escurra en un colador y enjuague con agua tibia. Al servir, vacíe la salsa y las albóndigas sobre el espagueti. Espolvoree el queso Parmesano si desea. Este platillo se complementa con ensalada, pan y vino.

★ 1 c. de hierbas secas finamente picadas equivale a 1 C. de hierbas frescas finamente picadas.

Pollo alla Galici (Chicken Galici)
Pollo Galici

鶏塊煮蛋麵

1

2

3

- Serves 4 -

10 oz. (280g) pkg. extra wide egg noodles (Fig. 1)

3 lbs. (1350g) frying chicken

1
- 1 c. $1/2$" (1 cm) diced onions
- 1 garlic clove, minced
- 1 $1/2$ T. finely diced dry basil leaves*
- 1 t. salt
- $1/4$ t. pepper

2
- 1 $1/2$ c. tomato sauce
- 1 c. water

1 c. water

- 4人份 -

寬蛋麵（圖1）
.............7兩（280公克）

鷄1隻 …2斤4兩（1350公克）

1
- 洋蔥（切丁）.................1杯
- 蒜（切碎）...................1瓣
- 碎乾九層塔* ....1 $1/2$大匙
- 鹽 1小匙
- 胡椒 ....$1/4$小匙

2
- 番茄調味汁 ....1 $1/2$杯
- 水 1杯

水 1杯

- 4 porciones -

10 oz. (280g) paquete de tallarines anchos (Fig. 1)

3 lbs. (1350g) pollo para freír

1
- 1 tz. cebolla picada en cubitos de $1/2$" (1 cm)
- 1 diente de ajo, finamente picado
- 1 $1/2$ C. hojas de albahaca secas finamente picadas*
- 1 c. sal
- $1/4$ c. pimienta

2
- 1 $1/2$ tz. salsa de tomate
- 1 tz. agua

1 tz. agua

---

1 Heat 4 T. olive oil in deep skillet over medium heat. Add noodles and fry until golden brown, stirring constantly. Remove and drain on paper towels (Fig. 2).

2 Cut chicken into 8 pieces (Fig. 3). (Remove skin if desired.) Wash and pat dry. Heat 3 T. oil in skillet over high heat. Fry chicken 15 minutes until brown on both sides. Remove chicken, add **1** and saute in juices over medium heat until onions are soft.

3 Return chicken to skillet, add **2**, mix well, bring to boil, lower heat, cover and simmer 30 minutes. Stir twice during simmer.

4 Add and stir in browned noodles and 1 c. water. Cover and cook 15 minutes, stirring occasionally, until noddles and chicken are done. Vegetables and bread go well with this dish.

★ 1 t. of finely diced dry herbs equals 1 T. of loosely packed finely diced fresh herbs.

---

1 橄欖油4大匙燒熱，用中火將蛋麵炒至金黃色撈出，置於紙巾上吸油（圖2）。

2 鷄切8塊（亦可去皮，圖3）洗淨，擦乾水份。油3大匙燒熱，用大火將鷄塊煎15分鐘至兩面均呈金黃色取出。

3 餘油用中火將 **1** 料炒至洋蔥軟，隨入鷄塊及 **2** 料拌勻燒開，改小火蓋鍋煮30分鐘（中途需翻拌）。

4 續入煎炸好的蛋麵及水1杯蓋鍋煮15分鐘（中途也需翻拌）至麵及鷄肉熟，可與蔬菜及麵包共食。

★ 碎乾九層塔1小匙相當於新鮮切碎的九層塔1大匙。

---

1 Caliente 4 C. de aceite de oliva en una cacerola honda a fuego moderado. Agregue los tallarines y fría hasta que se doren, revolviendo constantemente. Retire y escurra sobre toallas de papel (Fig. 2).

2 Corte el pollo en 8 piezas (Fig. 3). (Quítele la piel si lo desea.) Lave y seque ligeramente. Caliente 3 C. de aceite en una cacerola a fuego alto. Fría el pollo por 15 minutos hasta que se dore por ambos lados. Retire el pollo, agregue **1** y sofría en ese jugo a fuego moderado hasta que la cebolla esté blanda.

3 Regrese el pollo a la cacerola, agregue **2**, mezcle bien, haga hervir, baje el fuego, tape y cocine lentamente por 30 minutos. Revuelva dos veces mientras se cocina.

4 Agregue mezclando los tallarines dorados y 1 tz. de agua. Tape y cocine por 15 minutos, revolviendo ocasionalmente, hasta que los tallarines y el pollo estén cocidos. Este platillo se complementa con vegetales y pan.

★ 1 c. de hierbas secas finamente picadas equivale a 1 C. de hierbas frescas finamente picadas.

Cannelloni (Filled Pasta Tubes)
Cannelloni Rellenos

鑲麵筒

1

2

3

- Serves 4 -

1 | 3 c. spaghetti sauce
    (see p. 65, step 2)

8 cannelloni tubes (Fig. 1)

2 | $^1/_2$ lb. (225g) ground beef
  | 2 T. chopped onions

3 | $^1/_4$ t. salt, $^1/_8$ t. pepper
  | 1 egg, beaten
  | $^1/_4$ c. diced tomatoes
  | 1 T. finely diced dry parsley*
  | $^1/_2$ c. shredded Parmesan
  | cheese
  | $^1/_4$ c. finely diced fresh
  | spinach leaves

2 T. soft butter

4 | $^1/_8$ t. salt, $^1/_2$ c. milk

1 $^1/_2$ T. all-purpose flour

aluminum foil for baking

---

1 Prepare **1**, set aside. Put 6 c. water and 1 t. oil in pot and bring to boil, add tubes, cook 5 minutes until tender. Stir to prevent sticking. Remove with slotted spoon, rinse with warm water, drain and lay on cloth towel.

2 Place **2** (Fig. 2) in skillet over medium heat, break up meat into fine pieces and fry until brown. Remove heat, drain grease, add **3** and mix filling thoroughly. Fill each tube with 1/4 c. of meat filling (Fig. 3). Butter a 9" x 13" (22 cm x 32 cm) baking dish, pour 1 1/2 c. of **1** in bottom. Place filled tubes on sauce. Pour balance of **1** on top.

3 Prepare white sauce by melting butter over medium heat in pan. Mix in **4**, slowly add flour, stirring until sauce is smooth and starts to thicken. Spoon sauce evenly over each cannelloni. Loosely cover with foil, bake in preheated oven 350°F (180°C) 20 minutes. Goes well with vegetables.

★ 1 t. of finely diced herbs equals 1 T. loosely packed finely diced fresh herbs.

- 4人份 -

1 | 義大利麵醬（見65頁，作法2）
  | 3杯

通心麵筒（圖1）.........8個

2 | 牛絞肉 ....6兩（225公克）
  | 洋蔥（切丁）...........2大匙

3 | 鹽 $^1/_4$小匙，胡椒 ...$^1/_8$小匙
  | 蛋（打散）.............1個
  | 番茄（切丁）............$^1/_4$杯
  | 碎乾巴西利* 1大匙
  | 巴馬起士絲 ....$^1/_2$杯
  | 菠菜葉（切碎）..........$^1/_4$杯

奶油 2大匙

4 | 鹽...$^1/_8$小匙，牛奶 ...$^1/_2$杯

麵粉 ....1 $^1/_2$大匙

錫箔紙..................適量

---

1 將義大利麵醬做好備用。水6杯加油1小匙燒開，放入麵筒煮5分鐘至熟（煮時略攪，防止黏在一起）撈出並沖水瀝乾，置於布上吸去水份。

2 用中火將 **2** 料（圖2）炒開至肉變色，即熄火，倒出油，與 **3** 料拌勻成肉餡。每一個麵筒內填入 $^1/_4$ 杯的肉餡（圖3）。

3 將1 $^1/_2$ 杯的義大利麵醬澆在22公分×32公分塗有奶油的烤盤上；上置填好的麵筒，再澆入剩餘的義大利麵醬。

4 用中火將奶油在平底鍋內溶化，隨入 **4** 料並慢慢加入麵粉攪拌至汁呈濃稠狀，澆在麵筒上，蓋上錫箔紙（不必蓋緊）；烤箱燒熱，以350℉（180℃）烤20分鐘與蔬菜配食。

★ 碎乾香菜1小匙相當於新鮮切碎的香菜1大匙。

- 4 porciones -

1 | 3 tz. salsa de espagueti
  | (vea p. 65, paso 2)

8 tubos de cannelloni (Fig. 1)

2 | $^1/_2$ lb. (225g) carne de res
  | 2 C. cebolla picada

3 | $^1/_4$ c. sal, $^1/_8$ c. pimienta
  | 1 huevo, batido
  | $^1/_4$ tz. tomates picados en
  | cuadritos
  | 1 C. perejil seco finamente
  | picado*
  | $^1/_2$ tz. queso Parmesano rallado
  | $^1/_4$ tz. hojas de espinaca fresca
  | finamente picadas

2 C. mantequilla blanda

4 | $^1/_8$ c. sal, $^1/_2$ tz. leche

1 $^1/_2$ C. harina
papel de aluminio para
   hornear

---

1 Prepare **1**, deje aparte. Ponga 6 tz. de agua y 1 c. de aceite en una olla y haga hervir, agregue los tubos, cocine por 5 minutos hasta que se ablanden. Revuelva para que no se peguen. Sáquelos con una cuchara y enjuague con agua tibia, escurra y ponga sobre una toalla de cocina.

2 Ponga **2** (Fig. 2) en una cacerola a fuego moderado, desbarate la carne en pedazos chicos y fría hasta que se dore. Retire del fuego, escurra la grasa, agregue **3** y mezcle el relleno completamente. Rellene cada tubo con 1/4 tz. del relleno de carne (Fig. 3). Engrase un recipiente de hornear de 9" x 13" (22 cm x 32 cm), vacíe abajo 1 1/2 tz. de **1**. Coloque los fideos rellenos sobre la salsa. Vacíe lo restante de **1** encima.

3 Prepare la salsa blanca derritiendo la mantequilla a fuego alto en una sartén. Mézclele **4**, agregue la harina lentamente, revolviendo hasta que la salsa esté suave y empiece a espesarse. Vacíe la salsa con una cucharada sobre cada cannelloni en forma pareja. Tape con el aluminio flojamente, cocine en un horno precalentado a 350°F (180°C) por 20 minutos. Se complementan con vegetales.

★ 1 c. de hierbas secas finamente picadas equivale a 1 C. de hierbas frescas finamente picadas.

Calzone (Filled Pizza Turnover)
Empanadas de Pizza

麵包披薩

- Makes 4 -

1. | 2 1/4 t. (7g) active dry yeast
   | 1 t. sugar, 1/4 c. warm water

2. | 1/2 t. salt, 2/3 c. warm water
   | 2 T. olive oil

2 1/3 c. all-purpose flour

3. | 1 1/2 c. 1/2" (1 cm) diced cooked ham
   | 1 1/2 c. lightly chopped fresh spinach leaves
   | 2 c. sliced mushrooms
   | 2 c. shredded mozzarella cheese
   | 1/2 c. sliced black olives

extra flour and oil for handling
1 egg, beaten

1. Mix **1** in medium size bowl, let stand until foamy. Mix in **2** and flour. Place dough on floured surface, knead until smooth, put in greased bowl, turn to grease all sides. Cover, place in warm area, let rise 1 hour until double in size. While dough is rising, prepare filling **3** (Fig. 1) mixing thoroughly. Divide into 4 portions.

2. Place dough on floured surface, knead briefly and form into 4 balls. Flatten a ball by hand. Use rolling pin to shape into 8" (21 cm) circle. Place 1/4 of filling on dough leaving 1" (2.5 cm) clear for sealing (Fig. 2). Fold dough over the filling to form calzone. Seal by pressing edges together with fingers and then folding edges over (Fig. 3). Repeat step with each ball.

3. Place calzones on greased baking sheet. Brush egg over top of each calzone. Bake in pre-heated oven 400°F (200°C) 20 minutes until crust is golden. Spaghetti sauce (see p. 65, step 2) can be used on top if desired. Salad and wine go well with this dish.

- 4人份 -

1. | 酵母 ……………………2 1/4 小匙
   | 糖 …………………………1 小匙
   | 溫水 …………………………1/4 杯

2. | 鹽… 1/2 小匙，溫水 ……2/3 杯
   | 橄欖油 ……………………2 大匙

麵粉 …………………………2 1/3 杯

3. | 火腿（切丁）………………1 1/2 杯
   | 菠菜葉（略切）……………1 1/2 杯
   | 新鮮洋菇（切片）……………2 杯
   | 馬自拉起士絲 ………………2 杯
   | 黑橄欖（切片）……………1/2 杯

麵粉 ……………………………適量
油 ……………………………適量
蛋黃（打散）……………………1個

1. 將 **1** 料混合置中型碗內，待起泡後與 **2** 料、麵粉混合，揉成軟硬適中的麵糰。盆內塗油，放入麵糰，並翻面使表面沾到油，用布蓋住，置於溫暖的地方約1小時至麵糰發到二倍大。在等發麵中間將 **3** 料（圖1）混合成餡，分成四份備用。

2. 將發好的麵糰在撒有少許麵粉的板上略揉後分成四份壓扁，各擀成直徑21公分的大圓餅；每個圓餅各放入一份餡，留2.5公分邊緣做封口用（圖2）。將放有餡的圓餅對折成半圓形，封口用手指壓緊，再將邊緣折回成花邊（圖3），以免湯汁流出，同法做其他3個。

3. 將做好的餅置於塗油的烤盤上，塗上蛋液；烤箱燒熱，以400℉（200℃）烤20分鐘至金黃色。可澆上義大利麵醬（見65頁，作法2）與沙拉、酒共食。

- 4 porciones -

1. | 2 1/4 c. (7g) levadura fresca
   | 1 c. azúcar, 1/4 tz. agua tibia

2. | 1/2 c. sal, 2/3 tz. agua tibia
   | 2 C. aceite de oliva

2 1/3 tz. harina

3. | 1 1/2 tz. jamón cocido cortado en cubos de 1/2" (1 cm)
   | 1 1/2 tz. hojas de espinaca fresca picadas
   | 2 tz. hongos rebanados
   | 2 tz. queso Mozzarella rallado
   | 1/2 tz. aceitunas negras rebanadas

extra harina y aceite para amasar
1 huevo batido

1. En un tazón mediano mezcle **1**, deje aparte hasta que esté espumoso. Mézclelo con **2** y la harina. Ponga la masa en una superficie enharinada, amase hasta que esté suave, ponga en un tazón engrasado y revuelva para engrasarla totalmente. Tape y deje en un lugar caliente por 1 hora o hasta que doble su tamaño. Mientras la masa está subiendo, prepare el relleno **3** (Fig. 1) mezclando totalmente. Divida en 4 porciones.

2. Ponga la masa en la superficie enharinada, amase brevemente y forme 4 bolas. Aplaste cada bola con la mano. Use un rodillo para formar un círculo de 8" (21 cm). Ponga 1/4 del relleno en el centro de la masa dejando una orilla de 1" (2.5 cm) alrededor para cerrar (Fig. 2). Doble la masa sobre el relleno para formar la empanada. Para cerrar junte las orillas presionando con los dedos y doblando las orillas (Fig. 3). Repita el procedimiento con cada bola.

3. Ponga las empanadas en una charola engrasada. Con un cepillo unte con huevo cada empanada. Cocine en horno precalentado a 400°F (200°C) por 20 minutos hasta que estén dorados. Si lo desea puede ponerle arriba salsa de espagueti (vea p. 65, paso 2). Este platillo se complementa con ensalada y vino.

Lasagna di Carne (Meat Lasagna)
Lasaña de Carne

碎肉千層麵

- Serves 4 -

3 c. spaghetti sauce (see p. 65, step 2)
$1/2$ lb. (225g) ground beef
$1/2$ lb. (225g) 9 lasagna noodles (Fig. 1)

①
1 c. shredded mozzarella cheese
1 c. small curd cottage cheese or ricotta cheese
$1/2$ c. sour cream
$1/2$ t. salt

1 c. shredded mozzarella cheese

$1/4$ c. sliced black olives

aluminum foil for baking

1 Prepare sauce. Fry beef in skillet over medium heat until brown, drain grease. Add meat to sauce, set aside. Mix **①** (Fig. 2), set aside.

2 Place 6 c. water and 1 t. oil in pot, bring to boil, add noodles. Cook 6 minutes until tender stirring occasionally. Remove, rinse with warm water and drain. Lay flat on cloth towel, set aside.

3 Evenly spread 1 c. meat sauce in bottom of 7" x 11" (18 cm x 28 cm) baking dish. Place three noodles, slightly overlapping, on top of sauce. Spread half of **①** and 1/2 c. meat sauce over noodles (Fig. 3). Add second layer of three noodles, spread remainder of **①** and 1/2 c. meat sauce over second layer. Add a third layer of noodles and cover with remaining meat sauce.

4 Sprinkle cheese and top with olives. Cover with foil to seal and bake in preheated oven 350°F (180°C) 30 minutes until lasagna is thoroughly heated, remove. Let set 10 minutes before serving. Green vegetables or salad go well with this dish.

- 4人份 -

義大利麵醬（見65頁，作法2）
···························3杯

牛絞肉 ········6兩（225公克）

義大利麵板（圖1）
············6兩（225公克）

①
馬自拉起士絲（Mozzarella cheese）············1杯
鄉村起士或ricotta起士 ···1杯
酸奶油 ·····················$1/2$杯
鹽 ························$1/2$小匙

馬自拉起士絲 ············1杯
黑橄欖（切片）··········$1/4$杯
錫箔紙 ·····················適量

1 將義大利麵醬做好備用。用中火將肉炒到至變色，倒出油，與義大利麵醬拌勻成肉醬。**①**料（圖2）混合備用。

2 水6杯加油1小匙燒開，放入麵板煮6分鐘至熟（中途需攪拌）撈出，沖水瀝乾，平鋪在布上備用。

3 將1杯肉醬倒入18公分×28公分的烤盤底層，依次分層放入$1/3$的麵板，$1/2$的 **①** 料及$1/2$杯的肉醬一層層放入（圖3），同樣方法再做一次，最後鋪上第三層麵板，澆上剩餘的肉醬，上撒起士，以橄欖點綴，用錫箔紙蓋緊。

4 烤箱燒熱，以350℉（180℃）烤30分鐘至麵板熱取出，置10分鐘後與煮熟綠色蔬菜或沙拉配食。

- 4 porciones -

3 tz. salsa de espagueti (vea p. 65, paso 2)
$1/2$ lb. (225g) carne molida de res
$1/2$ lb. (225g) 9 fideos de lasaña (Fig. 1)

①
1 tz. queso Mozzarella rallado
1 tz. requesón o queso Ricotta
$1/2$ tz. crema agria
$1/2$ c. sal

1 tz. queso Mozzarella rallado

$1/4$ tz. aceitunas negras rebanadas

papel de aluminio para hornear

1 Prepare la salsa. Fría la carne en una cacerola a fuego moderado hasta que esté dorada, escurra la grasa. Agregue la carne a la salsa, deje aparte. Mezcle **①** (Fig. 2), deje aparte.

2 Ponga 6 tz. de agua y 1 c. de aceite en una olla, haga hervir, agregue los fideos. Cocine por 6 minutos, revolviendo ocasionalmente hasta que estén blandos. Retire, enjuague con agua tibia y cuélelos. Déjelos estirados en una toalla de cocina, deje aparte.

3 En forma pareja unte el fondo de un recipiente de hornear de 7" x 11" (18 cm x 28 cm) con la salsa de carne. Ponga 3 fideos arriba de la salsa. Esparza la mitad de **①** y 1/2 tz. de la salsa con carne sobre los fideos (Fig. 3). Agregue la segunda capa de 3 fideos, esparza encima el resto de **①** y 1/2 tz. de salsa con carne. Acomode la tercera capa de fideos y cubra con el resto de la salsa con carne.

4 Espolvoree el queso y encima ponga las aceitunas. Cubra totalmente con papel de aluminio y cocine en horno precalentado a 350°F (180°C) por 30 minutos hasta que la lasaña esté totalmente caliente, retire. Deje reposar por 10 minutos antes de servir. Este platillo se complementa con vegetales verdes o ensalada.

Zucchini Ripiene (Stuffed Zucchini)
Calabacitas Rellenas

鑲義大利瓜

1

2

3

- Serves 2 -

2 medium size (10 oz., 280g each) zucchinis (Fig. 1)

1 | ¹/₂ lb. (225g) ground beef
2 T. finely diced onions

2 | 2 t. finely diced dry parsley*
1 t. finely diced dry basil leaves*
¹/₄ t. salt
¹/₈ t. pepper
¹/₄ c. finely chopped tomato
¹/₄ c. dry bread crumbs, plain
¹/₄ c. grated Parmesan cheese

¹/₂ c. shredded mozzarella cheese

aluminum foil for baking

1 Wash and scrub zucchini, cut off ends and cut in half lengthwise. Scoop out pulp from each half (Fig. 1) leaving 1/4" (0.5 cm) thick shell. Finely dice pulp and set pulp and shells aside.

2 Place **1** in skillet over medium heat. Break up meat into fine pieces and fry until brown. Drain grease. Add **2** (Fig. 2), diced pulp, and 2 T. water. Mix thoroughly.

3 Fill each zucchini shell with 1/4 of mixture **2** . Place filled zucchini shells skin-side down on buttered 2 qt. 8" x 8" (21 cm x 21 cm) baking dish (Fig. 3). Sprinkle with cheese, loosely cover with foil and bake in preheated oven at 350°F (180°C) for 20 minutes. Remove foil and bake 10 more minutes until filling and cheese is lightly browned.

★ 1 t. of finely diced dry herbs equal 1 T. of loosely packed finely diced fresh herbs.

- 2人份 -

義大利瓜（圖1，中2條）
　　　……… 7.5兩（280公克）

1 | 牛絞肉 ……… 6兩（225公克）
洋蔥（切碎）…………… 2大匙

2 | 碎乾巴西利* ……… 2小匙
碎乾九層塔* ……… 1小匙
鹽 ……………………… ¹/₄小匙
胡椒 …………………… ¹/₈小匙
番茄（切丁）………… ¹/₄杯
麵包粉 ………………… ¹/₄杯
碎巴馬起士 …………… ¹/₄杯

馬自拉起士絲 ………… ¹/₂杯

錫箔紙 ………………… 適量

1 義大利瓜洗淨，去頭尾，切半，挖出果肉（圖1）留0.5公分厚殼，果肉切碎後備用。

2 用中火將 **1** 料炒開至肉變色，倒出油，隨入 **2** 料（圖2）、碎果肉及水2大匙拌勻成餡。

3 在每個瓜殼內鑲入 ¹/₄ 的餡，皮向下置於21公分×21公分塗有奶油的烤盤肉（圖3），上撒起士絲，蓋上錫箔紙（不必蓋緊）；烤箱燒熱，以350 ℉（180℃）烤20分鐘，不加蓋續烤10分鐘至表面呈棕色。

★ 碎乾香菜1小匙相當於新鮮切碎的香菜1大匙。

- 2 porciones -

2 calabacitas medianas (10 oz., 280g c/u) (Fig. 1)

1 | ¹/₂ lb. (225g) carne molida de res
2 C. cebolla, finamente picada

2 | 2 c. perejil seco finamente picado*
1 c. hojas de albahaca seca finamente picada*
¹/₄ c. sal
¹/₈ c. pimienta
¹/₄ tz. tomates finamente picados
¹/₄ tz. pan seco molido
¹/₄ tz. queso Parmesano rallado

¹/₂ tz. queso Mozzarella rallado

papel de aluminio para hornear

1 Lave y restriegue las calabacitas, córtele los extremos y córtelas a lo largo por la mitad. Saque la pulpa de cada mitad (Fig. 1) dejándolas de 1/4" (0.5 cm) de grosor. Pique finamente la pulpa, déjela aparte y también las calabacitas.

2 Ponga **1** en una cacerola a fuego moderado. Desbarate la carne y fría hasta que se dore. Escurra la grasa. Agregue **2** (Fig. 2), la pulpa picada y 2 C. de agua. Mezcle completamente.

3 Rellene cada calabacita con 1/4 de la mezcla **2** . Ponga las calabacitas rellenas con la cáscara abajo en un recipiente enmantequillado de hornear de 2 litros, 8" x 8" (21 cm x 21 cm) (Fig 3). Espolvoree el queso. Tape sin sellar con el papel de aluminio y cocine en horno precalentado a 350°F (180°C) por 20 minutos. Quítele el aluminio y cocine 10 minutos más hasta que el queso esté ligeramente dorado.

★ 1 c. de hierbas secas finamente picadas equivale a 1 C. de hierbas frescas finamente picadas.

Pollo alla Cacciatora (Chicken and Vegetables)
Pollo con Vegetales

蔬菜燒鷄

1

2

3

- Serves 4 -

1 ½ lbs. (675g) skinned boneless chicken breasts

¼ c. all-purpose flour

1
½ lb. (225g) fresh mushroom caps, cut in half
1 c. ³/₄" (2 cm) chopped onions
1 garlic clove, minced (optional)
1 t. salt
½ t. pepper

2
2 c. ³/₄" (2 cm) chopped tomatoes
2 medium-size carrots, cut into ¼" (0.5 cm) slices
1 large green bell pepper, ³/₄" (2 cm) chopped
1 t. finely diced dry basil leaves*
2 T. finely diced dry parsley*

3
½ c. ea: canned ready-to-serve chicken broth, dry white wine

2 small zucchinis cut into ¼" (0.5 cm) slices

1 Wash chicken, pat dry, cut into large bite-size pieces, (Fig. 1) and lightly flour. Heat 3 T. olive oil in deep skillet over high heat. Fry chicken, turning until all sides are brown. Remove chicken, add **1** (Fig. 2) and saute in juices over medium heat (add oil if needed), until onions are soft and slightly brown.

2 Add **2** (Fig. 3) and **3** to skillet and stir. Add fried chicken, bring to boil, reduce heat, cover and simmer 20 minutes. Stir twice during cooking. Add zucchini, mix well and simmer 10 more minutes. Warm rolls or bread go well with this meal.

★ 1 t. of finely diced dry herbs equals 1 T. loosely packed finely diced fresh herbs.

- 4人份 -

去皮雞胸肉1斤2兩（675公克）

麵粉‥‥‥‥‥‥‥‥‥¼杯

1
新鮮洋菇（切半）
‥‥‥‥‥6兩（225公克）
洋蔥（切小塊）‥‥‥‥‥1杯
蒜（切碎，無亦可）‥‥‥1瓣
鹽‥‥‥‥‥‥‥‥‥‥1小匙
胡椒‥‥‥‥‥‥‥‥‥½小匙

2
番茄（切小塊）‥‥‥‥‥2杯
紅蘿蔔（中，切片）‥‥‥2條
青椒（大，切小塊）‥‥‥1個
碎乾九層塔*‥‥‥‥‥‥1小匙
碎乾巴西利*‥‥‥‥‥‥2大匙

3
罐頭雞湯**（內含鹽）‥½杯
白酒‥‥‥‥‥‥‥‥‥½杯

義大利瓜（小，切片）‥‥2條

1 肉洗淨，擦乾水份，切大塊（圖1）在表面撒少許麵粉。橄欖油3大匙燒熱，用大火將肉煎至兩面呈金黃色撈出。餘油用中火炒 **1** 料（圖2）至洋蔥軟呈淡黃色。

2 隨入 **2** 料（圖3）、**3** 料略炒，續入肉塊燒開，改小火蓋鍋煮20分鐘（中途需翻拌），再加義大利瓜拌勻煮10分鐘與麵包共食。

★ 碎乾香菜1小匙相當於新鮮切碎的香菜1大匙。

★★ 若使用一般自製高湯可酌加鹽¼小匙。

■ 此道菜葷、蔬齊全，燴飯、燴麵均不錯，**3** 料內的白酒可用米酒取代。

- 4 porciones -

1 ½ lb. (675g) pechugas de pollos, deshuesadas y sin piel
¼ tz. harina

1
½ lb. (225g) cabecitas de hongos frescos, cortadas por la mitad
1 tz. cebolla cortada en ³/₄" (2 cm)
1 diente de ajo, finamente picado (opcional)
1 c. sal
½ c. pimienta

2
2 tz. tomates picados en ³/₄" (2 cm)
2 zanahorias medianas cortadas en rebanadas de ¼" (0.5 cm)
1 pimiento verde grande picado ³/₄" (2 cm)
1 c. hojas de albahaca seca*, finamente picada
2 C. perejil seco, finamente picado*

3
½ tz. c/u: caldo de pollo enlatado (listo para servir), vino blanco seco

2 calabacitas chicas cortadas en rebanadas de ¼" (0.5 cm)

1 Lave el pollo, seque ligeramente, córtelo en pedazos grandes tamaño bocado, (Fig. 1) y enharínelos ligeramente. Caliente 3 C. de aceite de oliva en una cacerola honda a fuego alto. Fría el pollo volteando hasta que se dore completamente. Retire el pollo, agregue **1** (Fig. 2) y sofría en ese jugo a fuego moderado, (agregue aceite si es necesario) hasta que las cebollas estén blandas y levemente doradas.

2 Agregue **2** (Fig. 3) y **3** a la cacerola y revuelva. Agregue el pollo frito, haga hervir, baje el fuego, tape y cocine lentamente por 20 minutos. Revuelva dos veces mientras se cocina. Agregue las calabacitas, mezcle bien y cocine 10 minutos más. Esta comida se complementa con pan o bolillos calientes.

★ 1 c. de hierbas secas finamente picadas equivale a 1 C. de hierbas frescas finamente picadas.

Lime Chicken (Chicken Larb)
Pollo con Limón Verde

檸檬碎鷄肉

1

2

3

- Serves 2 -

²/₃ lb. (300g) minced boneless chicken, (Fig. 1) or ground beef or tuna

1
2 T. fish sauce (see p. 90, Fig. 1)
3 T. lime juice

2
¹/₂ t. chili powder
1 t. galangal powder (Fig. 2)
1 T. ground rice*
¹/₂ c. shredded red onion
¹/₂ c. minced green onion
¹/₂ c. minced coriander
2 kaffir leaves or mint leaves, shredded

1 Stir-fry meat in a small pan with no oil or water until cooked; turn off heat immediately. Mix with **1** first then **2** (Fig. 3).

★ Ground Rice: Stir-fry uncooked rice gently until it turns brown then grind into fine pieces (ready-made ground rice may be purchased in most markets).

■ This dish is low in fat and has a sweet and sour taste. It is suitable for salads, appetizers, or when served with rice or lettuce.

- 2人份 -

鷄肉（剁碎，圖1）或牛絞肉 或鮪魚 …半斤（300公克）

1
魚露（見90頁，圖1）…2大匙
靑檸檬汁 …………………3大匙

2
辣椒粉 …………………¹/₂小匙
南羌粉（圖2）…………1小匙
碎米* …………………1大匙
紅洋蔥（切絲）…………¹/₂杯
蔥（切碎）………………¹/₂杯
香菜（切碎）……………¹/₂杯
泰國檸檬葉或薄荷葉（切絲）
…………………………2片

1 將肉放入無油無水的小鍋內炒 開至熟，立即熄火，先拌 **1** 料 再拌 **2** 料（圖3）即成。

★ 碎米即生米在乾鍋內慢炒至淡 黃色取出壓碎而成（市面上有 現成的出售）。

■ 此道菜爲低脂肪並帶酸辣口 味，經常作爲沙拉或開胃菜， 或與飯、生菜配食。

- 2 porciones -

²/₃ lb. (300g) pollo sin hueso, desmenuzado (Fig. 1) o carne molida de res o atún

1
2 C. salsa de pescado (vea p. 90, Fig. 1)
3 C. jugo de limón verde

2
¹/₂ c. chile en polvo
1 c. polvo galangal (Fig. 2)
1 C. arroz molido*
¹/₂ tz. cebolla colorada rallada
¹/₂ tz. cebollín finamente picado
¹/₂ tz. cilantro finamente picado
2 hojas de kaffir o hierba buena, finamente picadas

1 Fría-revolviendo la carne en una sartén chica sin agua o aceite hasta que se cocine; apague el fuego de inmediato. Primero mezcle con **1**, luego **2** (Fig. 3).

★ Arroz Molido: Fría-revolviendo arroz crudo hasta que se dore luego muela en pedazos finos (puede comprar arroz molido ya preparado en la mayoría de los mercados).

■ Este platillo es bajo en calorías y tiene un sabor agridulce. Se complementa con ensaladas, botanas, o con arroz o lechuga.

Green Curry Beef & Eggplant
Res con Curry Verde y Berenjena

緑咖哩煮牛肉茄子

1

2

3

- Serves 2 -

1
- 2 T. green curry paste (Fig. 1)
- ¹/₂ c. coconut milk* (or milk)
- 1 T. oil

2
- ¹/₂ lb. (225g) beef or boneless chicken, sliced
- 6 kaffir leaves (Fig. 2)
- 1 T. palm sugar (see p. 84, Fig. 1) or brown sugar
- 1 ¹/₂ c. coconut milk* (or milk)
- 2 T. fish sauce (see p. 90, Fig. 1)

3
- ¹/₃ lb. (150g) Japanese eggplant, cut in 1" (2.5 cm) cubes
- 1 c. sliced bamboo shoots
- ¹/₂ c. fresh basil leaves (see p. 86, Fig. 2)

2 c. cooked rice

1. Cook and stir **1** over medium heat 3 minutes until fragrant. Add **2** ; bring to boil. Add **3** , and bring to another boil; continue to cook 5 minutes.

2. Put rice in 2 serving bowls; top with meat and eggplant. Serve.

★ Coconut milk: Mix 2 c. grated coconut with 3 c. of hot water then puree in a blender. Filter the mixture. After refrigerating (Fig. 3), combine all the thick coconut milk that is floating on top with a portion of the coconut milk at the bottom to make 2 cups.

- 2人份 -

1
- 綠咖哩醬（圖1）·········2大匙
- 椰奶*（或牛奶）··········¹/₂杯
- 油 ···················1大匙

2
- 牛或鷄肉（切片）
　　　······6兩（225公克）
- 泰國檸檬葉（圖2）········6片
- 椰子糖（見84頁，圖1）或黑糖 ················1大匙
- 椰奶*（或牛奶）········1 ¹/₂杯
- 魚露（見90頁，圖1）···2大匙

3
- 茄子（切2公分正方塊）
　　　·········4兩（150公克）
- 筍（切片）···············1杯
- 九層塔（見86頁，圖2）¹/₂杯

飯 ···················2碗

1. 將 **1** 料用中火邊攪邊煮至有香味約3分鐘，隨入 **2** 料以大火燒開，加 **3** 料再燒開，續煮5分鐘即可。

2. 盤內盛飯，上置煮好的牛肉茄子，即可食用。

★ 椰奶做法：椰子粉2杯加熱水3杯，用果汁機攪爛後過濾，放入冰箱內冷藏後（圖3），將浮在上面的全部椰奶漿及下面的部份椰奶水取出共2杯使用。

- 2 porciones -

1
- 2 C. pasta de curry verde (Fig. 1)
- ¹/₂ tz. leche de coco* (o leche)
- 1 C. aceite

2
- ¹/₂ lb. (225g) res o pollo sin hueso, rebanado
- 6 hojas de kaffir (Fig. 2)
- 1 C. azúcar de palma (vea p. 84, Fig. 1) o azúcar morena
- 1¹/₂ tz. leche de coco* (o leche)
- 2 C. salsa de pescado (vea p. 90, Fig. 1)

3
- ¹/₃ lb. 150g) berenjena japonesa, cortada en cubos de 1" (2.5 cm)
- 1 tz. brotes de bambú rebanados
- ¹/₂ tz. hojas frescas de albahaca (vea p. 86, Fig. 2)

2 tz. arroz cocido

1. 1. Cocine y revuelva **1** a fuego moderado por 3 minutos hasta que esté aromático. Agregue **2** ; haga hervir. Agregue **3** , y haga hervir de nuevo, continúe cocinando por 5 minutos.

2. Ponga el arroz en 2 tazones a servir; cubra con la carne y la berenjena. Sirva.

★ Leche de coco: Mezcle 2 tz. de coco rallado con 3 tz. de agua caliente luego haga un puré en la licuadora. Cuele la mezcla. Después de refrigerar (Fig. 3) combine toda la leche espesa de coco que está flotando arriba con una parte de la leche de coco que está abajo para hacer 2 tazas.

Fried Thai Noodles (Pad Thai)
Fideos Thai Fritos

泰式炒麵

1

2

3

- Serves 2 -	**- 2人份 -**	**- 2 porciones -**

¹/₃ lb. (150g) dried Thai noodles (Fig. 1) or thin rice noodles

乾泰國麵（圖1）或米粉
·············4兩（150公克）

¹/₃ lb. (150g) fideos thai secos (Fig. 1) o fideos de arroz delgados

1
4 garlic cloves, minced
¹/₄ c. dried shrimp, rinsed

1
蒜（切碎）·············4瓣
蝦米（略洗）·············¹/₄杯

1
4 dientes de ajo, finamente picados
¹/₄ tz. camarón seco, enjuagado

2
¹/₂ c. baked bean curd, diced
5 T. toasted or fried peanuts, crushed
1 t. ground dried chili pepper

2
豆腐干（切丁）·············¹/₂杯
烤或炸花生（壓碎）·····5大匙
辣椒粉 ·············1小匙

2
¹/₂ tz. tofu cocido, cortado en cubos
5 C. cacahuates dorados o fritos, machacados
1 c. chile seco molido

3
2 ¹/₂ T. each: brown sugar, fish sauce (see p. 90, Fig. 1)
3 T. lime juice

3
黑糖、魚露（見90頁，圖1）
·············各2¹/₂大匙
青檸檬汁 ·············3大匙

3
2¹/₂ C. c/u: azúcar morena, salsa de pescado (vea p. 90, Fig. 1)
3 C. jugo de limón verde

2 eggs (beaten)

蛋（打散）·············2個

2 huevos batidos

4
4 green onions, cut 2" (5 cm) long
¹/₃ lb. (150g) bean sprouts

4
蔥（切5公分長）·············4支
豆芽菜 ·······4兩（150公克）

4
4 cebollines, cortados en pedazos de 2" (5 cm) de largo
¹/₃ lb. (150g) brotes de soya

---

1 Soak Thai noodles in water to yield 1/2 lb. (225g). Set aside. (Also, if using rice noodles soak in water).

2 Heat 5 T. oil. Stir-fry **1** (Fig. 2) until fragrant; add noodles and stir-fry until hot. Add **2** (Fig. 3) and mixture **3** ; stir to mix well then move to the side of the wok. Stir-fry eggs until slightly solidified. Add **4** and return the noodles; stir to mix well. Serve.

■ This is the most common Thai noodle dish. It is cooked by street vendors, and can be found on almost every corner along the streets of Bangkok. Pad Thai has now become one of the best known noodle dishes in Los Angeles.

1 乾泰國麵用水泡軟後約6兩（225公克）備用（若用米粉也需用水泡軟）。

2 油5大匙燒熱，炒香 **1** 料（圖2），隨入麵炒熱，再加 **2** 料（圖3）及調勻的 **3** 料炒拌均勻，鏟於鍋邊，入蛋炒至剛熟，加 **4** 料連同麵全部拌勻即成。

■ 此為泰國最普遍的炒麵，曼谷街邊的攤販都有販賣，目前在洛杉磯也是眾所皆知的麵點。

1 Remoje los fideos thai en agua para obtener 1/2 lb. (225g). Deje aparte (si usa fideos de arroz, también remójelos en agua).

2 Caliente 5 C. de aceite. Fría-revolviendo **1** (Fig. 2) hasta que esté aromático; agregue el fideo y fría-revolviendo hasta que se caliente. Agregue **2** (Fig. 3) y la mezcla **3** ; revuelva mezclando bien y haga a un lado de la wok. Fría-revolviendo los huevos hasta que estén un poco cuajados. Agregue **4** y los fideos; revuelva mezclando completamente. Sirva.

■ Este es el platillo más común de fideo thai. Es cocinado por vendedores ambulantes, y lo puede encontrar en casi todas las esquinas de las calles de Bangkok. Pad Thai ahora es uno de los platillos más conocidos en Los Ángeles.

Fried Rice & Sweet Meat (Kao Klook Ka Pi)

Arroz Frito y Carne Dulce

炒飯與甜肉

- Serves 2 -

1. | 2 eggs
   | 2 t. fish paste

2. | $^1/_2$ lb. (225g) lean meat (pork, beef or chicken), cut in strips
   | 1 $^1/_2$ T. ginger (minced)

3. | 1 $^1/_3$ T. fish sauce (see p. 90, Fig. 1)
   | 1 $^1/_3$ T. palm sugar (Fig, 1) or brown sugar
   | 1 $^1/_3$ t. dark soy sauce (see p. 12, Fig. 2)

4. | 2 cloves of garlic, minced
   | $^1/_4$ c. each: red onions (minced), dried shrimp (rinsed)
   | 1 t. shrimp paste (da-pi) (Fig. 2)

2 c. cooked rice

$^1/_4$ c. chopped green onions

1. Spread oil on the surface of wok. Fry mixture **1** to form a pancake; remove and shred.

2. Heat 2 T. oil. Add **2** (Fig. 3); stir-fry until separated and cooked. Add mixture **3**; stir-fry until partially evaporated; remove.

3. Heat 2 T. oil. Stir-fry **4** until fragrant (stir-fry shrimp paste thoroughly to prevent forming solid particles and to create a special flavor); add rice and stir-fry to mix well. Sprinkle on onions; serve.

4. Put rice, eggs and meat in 2 serving bowls. Sprinkle with lime juice as desired. Serve with cucumbers, coriander and chili.

- 2人份 -

2. | 蛋 ·············2個
   | 魚露 ·············2小匙

2. | 瘦肉（豬、牛或雞）
   | ········切條6兩（225公克）
   | 薑（切碎） ·········1 $^1/_2$大匙

3. | 魚露（見90頁，圖1）1 $^1/_3$大匙
   | 椰子糖（圖1）或黑糖1 $^1/_3$大匙
   | 老抽（深色醬油見12頁，圖2）
   | ·············1 $^1/_3$小匙

4. | 蒜（切碎）·············2瓣
   | 紅洋蔥（切碎）、蝦米（略洗）
   | ·············各 $^1/_4$杯
   | 蝦醬（圖2）·········1小匙

飯 ·············2碗

蔥花 ·············$^1/_4$杯

1. 將少量油塗一層在鍋面，放入打散的 **1** 料煎成蛋餅，取出切絲。

2. 油2大匙燒熱，放入 **2** 料（圖3）炒開至熟，隨入調勻的 **3** 料炒拌至汁略收乾即起。

3. 油2大匙燒熱，炒香 **4** 料（炒時須將蝦醬炒開，以免結顆粒；蝦醬炒後有奇特香味），隨入飯炒拌均勻，撒上蔥花即成。

4. 盤內盛炒飯、蛋及肉，可略撒青檸檬汁並與黃瓜、香菜、辣椒配食。

- 2 porciones -

1. | 2 huevos
   | 2 c. pasta de pescado

2. | $^1/_2$ lb. (225g) carne magra (cerdo, res o pollo) cortada en tiras
   | 1$^1/_2$ C. jengibre (finamente picado)

3. | 1$^1/_3$ C. salsa de pescado (vea p. 90, Fig. 1)
   | 1$^1/_3$ C. azúcar de palma (Fig. 1) o azúcar morena
   | 1$^1/_3$ c. salsa de soya oscura (vea p. 12, Fig. 2)

4. | 2 dientes de ajo, finamente picados
   | $^1/_4$ tz. c/u: cebolla colorada (finamente picada), camarones secos (enjuagados)
   | 1 c. pasta de camarones (da-pi) (Fig. 2)

2 tz. arroz cocido

$^1/_4$ tz. cebolla verde picada

1. Unte la sartén wok con aceite. Fría la mezcla **1** para hacer un panqueque; retire y córtelo en tiras.

2. Caliente 2 C. de aceite. Agregue **2** (Fig. 3); fría-revolviendo hasta que esté separado y cocido. Agregue la mezcla **3**; fría-revolviendo hasta que esté parcialmente evaporado, retire.

3. Caliente 2 C. de aceite. Fría-revolviendo **4** hasta que esté aromático (fría-revolviendo la pasta de camarones completamente para prevenir que se formen grumos y para conseguir un sabor especial); agregue el arroz y fría-revolviendo para mezclar bien. Esparza la cebolla; sirva.

4. Ponga el arroz, huevos y carne en 2 tazones a servir. Rocíe con jugo de limón verde, al gusto. Sirva con pepinos, cilantro y chile.

Spicy Meat & Basil on Rice
Carne Picante y Albahaca Sobre Arroz

辣椒絞肉燴飯

- Serves 2 -

²/₃ lb. (300g) ground pork, beef or chicken

1
- 1 t. red wine or rice wine
- 1 t. oyster sauce (Fig. 1)
- 1 t. cornstarch

2
- 4 cloves of garlic, minced
- 4 serrano chilies, minced
- ¹/₂ c. onions, minced

3
- 1 T. oyster sauce (Fig. 1)
- 1 T. fish sauce (see p. 90, Fig. 1)
- 1 T. dark soy sauce (see p. 12, Fig. 2)
- 1 c. fresh basil leaves (Fig. 2)

2 c. cooked rice

- 2人份 -

絞肉（豬、牛或雞）
‥‥‥‥‥半斤（300公克）

1
- 紅葡萄酒（或米酒）‥‥‥1小匙
- 蠔油（圖1）‥‥‥‥‥‥1小匙
- 玉米粉 ‥‥‥‥‥‥‥‥1小匙

2
- 蒜（切碎）‥‥‥‥‥‥4瓣
- 辣椒（切碎）‥‥‥‥‥4支
- 洋蔥（切碎）‥‥‥‥‥¹/₂杯

3
- 蠔油（圖1）‥‥‥‥‥‥1大匙
- 魚露（見90頁，圖1）‥‥1大匙
- 老抽（深色醬油見12頁，圖2）
  ‥‥‥‥‥‥‥‥‥‥1大匙
- 九層塔（圖2）‥‥‥‥‥1杯

飯 ‥‥‥‥‥‥‥‥‥‥2碗

- 2 porciones -

²/₃ lb. (300g) carne molida de cerdo, res o pollo

1
- 1 c. vino tinto o vino de arroz
- 1 c. salsa de ostras (Fig. 1)
- 1 c. maicena

2
- 4 dientes de ajo, finamente picados
- 4 chiles serranos, finamente picados
- ¹/₂ tz. cebolla, finamente picada

3
- 1 C. salsa de ostras (Fig. 1)
- 1 C. salsa de pescado (vea p. 90, Fig. 1)
- 1 C. salsa de soya oscura (vea p. 12, Fig. 2)
- 1 tz. hojas de albahaca fresca (Fig. 2)

2 tz. arroz cocido.

---

1 Mix ground meat with **1** well.

2 Heat 4 T. oil. Stir-fry **2** (Fig. 3) until fragrant; add ground meat then stir-fry until separated and cooked. Add mixture **3** and stir-fry; add 1/2 c. water and bring to boil.

3 Put rice in 2 serving bowls, top with spicy ground meat. Serve with poached egg and cucumber as desired.

■ This dish is easy to make and tastes great; ideal for busy working people with little spare time.

---

1 絞肉調 **1** 料拌勻。

2 油4大匙燒熱，炒香 **2** 料（圖3），隨入絞肉炒開至熟，加入調勻的 **3** 料炒拌，再加水¹/₂杯燒開即成。

3 盤內盛飯，上置炒好的辣椒絞肉，隨意與煎荷包蛋及黃瓜配食。

■ 此為簡易又可口的菜餚，非常適合忙碌的上班族。

---

1 Mezcle bien la carne con **1** .

2 Caliente 4 C. de aceite. Fría-revolviendo **2** (Fig. 3) hasta que esté aromático; agregue la carne molida. Fría-revolviendo hasta que la carne esté separada y cocida. Agregue la mixtura **3** y fría-revolviendo, agregue 1/2 tz. de agua y haga hervir.

3 Ponga el arroz en dos tazones a servir, acomode encima la carne molida. Sirva con huevo escalfado y pepino si lo desea.

■ Este platillo es fácil de preparar y su sabor es delicioso, lo ideal para gente ocupada con poco tiempo para cocinar.

Sauteed Chicken & Vegetables on Rice
Pollo Sofrito y Vegetales Sobre Arroz

鮮蔬肉片燴飯

- Serves 2 -	- 2人份 -	- 2 porciones -
½ lb. (225g) boneless chicken, beef or pork, sliced	鶏、牛或豬肉（切片） …………6兩（225公克）	½ lb. (225g) pollo deshuesado, res o cerdo, rebanado
1 ⅔ T. oyster sauce ⅔ T. cooking wine ⅔ T. cornstarch	**1** 蠔油 …………⅔大匙 酒 …………⅔大匙 玉米粉 …………⅔大匙	**1** ⅔ C. salsa de ostras ⅔ C. vino para cocinar ⅔ C. maicena
1 T. minced garlic	蒜（切碎）…………1大匙	1 C. ajo, finamente picado
2 1 t. sugar ½ t. white pepper 1 T. oyster sauce 2 T. white soy sauce (Fig. 1) ½ T. vinegar	**2** 糖 …………1小匙 白胡椒 …………½小匙 蠔油 …………1大匙 淡醬油（圖1）…………2大匙 醋 …………½大匙	**2** 1 c. azúcar ½ c. pimienta blanca 1 C. salsa de ostras 2 C. salsa de soya blanca (Fig. 1) ½ C. vinagre
3 2 Chinese black mushrooms (presoftened, shredded) ½ c. canned straw mushrooms 1 c. nappa cabbage, cut in pieces	**3** 香菇（泡軟，切絲）…………2朵 草菇（罐頭）…………½杯 白菜（切塊）…………1杯	**3** 2 hongos negros chinos (previamente remojados y rebanados) ½ tz. hongos enlatados (straw mushrooms) 1 tz. repollo napa, cortado en pedazos
4 ½ c. asparagus, cut 2" (5 cm) long ¼ c. onion or green onion, cut 2" (5 cm) long 3 chili peppers, sliced	**4** 蘆筍（切5公分長）…………½杯 洋蔥或蔥（切5公分長）…¼杯 辣椒（切片）…………3支	**4** ½ tz. espárragos, cortados en 2" (5cm) de largo ¼ tz. cebolla o cebollín, cortado en 2" (5cm) de largo 3 chiles, rebanados
5 1 T. cornstarch ¾ c. water	**5** 玉米粉 …………1大匙 水 …………¾杯	**5** 1 C. maicena ¾ tz. agua
2 c. cooked rice	飯 …………2碗	2 tz. arroz cocido

1 Mix meat with ① well.

2 Heat 3 T. oil. Stir-fry garlic until fragrant. Add meat slices; stir-fry until separated and cooked. Add ②, then ③, ④ (Figs. 2 & 3), and mixture ⑤; stir-fry to mix. Cover, bring to boil, and briefly stir-fry until mixed well.

3 Put cooked rice or noodles on 2 serving plates, top with cooked vegetables and meat slices. Serve.

1 肉片調 ① 料拌勻備用。

2 油3大匙燒熱，炒香蒜，隨入肉片炒開至熟，拌入 ② 料並加 ③ 、 ④ 料（圖2、3）及調勻的 ⑤ 料炒拌，蓋鍋燒開再略炒均勻即成。

3 盤肉盛飯或麵，上置炒好的鮮蔬肉片即可食用。

■ 此菜餚有肉有蔬菜，口味爲泰菜與中國菜之結合，多種蔬菜看來複雜，但可集合冰箱內現有的多種顏色蔬菜搭配使用，做法簡單可口，值得一試。

1 Mezcle bien la carne con ①.

2 Caliente 3 C. de aceite. Fría-revolviendo el ajo hasta que esté aromático. Agregue las rebanadas de carne; fría-revolviendo hasta que la carne esté separada y cocida. Agregue ②, luego ③, ④ (Figs. 2 y 3), y la mezcla ⑤; fría-revolviendo para mezclar. Tape, haga hervir y brevemente fría-revolviendo para mezclar bien.

3 Ponga el arroz o fideos en los dos platos a servir, acomode encima los vegetales cocidos y la carne. Sirva.

Pork Stew on Rice
Estofado de Cerdo Sobre Arroz

鹹菜紅燒肉燴飯

1

2

3

1 lb. (450g) boneless chicken legs or pork

1
- 1 T. oyster sauce
- 1 T. dark soy sauce (see p. 12, Fig. 2)
- 1 T. cornstarch

2
- 1/4 c. minced garlic
- 1/4 c. minced coriander
- 1 t. pepper

3
- 1/3 lb. (150g) pickled mustard cabbage, cut in pieces
- 1/2 lb. (225g) Chinese broccoli or nappa cabbage, cut in pieces

4
- 1 T. sugar
- 1 T. fish sauce (Fig. 1)
- 3 c. water

2 c. cooked rice

1 Cut pork in pieces (Fig. 2); mix with **1** well.

2 Heat 3 T. oil. Stir-fry meat until it turns yellowish; add **2** and stir-fry until fragrant. Add **3** (Fig. 3); stir-fry briefly. Add **4**; bring to boil. Reduce heat to medium and stew uncovered 45 minutes. Stir during cooking until the sauce is partially evaporated.

3 Put rice on 2 serving plates; top with meat. May serve with vegetables.

■ This dish is very appetizing because of the flavor from the pickled mustard cabbage. Due to the long cooking time, this dish may be prepared and cooked in advance.

豬腿肉或鷄腿肉
　　　　　……12兩（450公克）

1
蠔油 ……………………1大匙
老抽（深色醬油，見12頁，圖2）
玉米粉 …………………1大匙

2
蒜（切碎）……………1/4杯
香菜莖（切碎）………1/4杯
胡椒 ……………………1小匙

3
鹹酸菜（切塊）4兩（150公克）
芥蘭菜或白菜（切塊）
　　　　　……6兩（225公克）

3
糖 ………………………1大匙
魚露（圖1）……………1大匙
水 ………………………3杯

飯 ………………………2碗

1 豬腿肉切塊（圖2），調 **1** 料拌勻備用。

2 油3大匙燒熱，將肉煎炒至淡黃色，隨入 **2** 料炒香，續入 **3** 料（圖3）略炒，再加 **4** 料燒開改中火不蓋鍋煮45分鐘，中途需翻拌至汁略收乾。

3 盤內盛飯，上置紅燒肉，可與蔬菜配食。

■ 此道菜因有鹹酸菜，非常下飯；但燒煮時間長，可預先煮好備用。

---

1 lb. (450g) piernas deshuesadas de pollo o cerdo

1
- 1 C. salsa de ostras
- 1 C. salsa de soya oscura (vea p. 12, Fig. 2)
- 1 C. maicena

2
- 1/4 tz. ajo, finamente picado
- 1/4 tz. cilantro, finamente picado
- 1 c. pimienta

3
- 1/3 lb. (150g) repollo mostaza escabechado, cortado en pedazos
- 1/2 lb. (225g) bróculi chino o repollo napa, cortado en pedazos

4
- 1 C. azúcar
- 1 C. salsa de pescado (Fig. 1)
- 3 tz. agua

2 tz. arroz cocido

1 1. Corte el cerdo en pedazos (Fig. 2); mezcle bien con **1**.

2 Caliente 3 C. de aceite. Fría-revolviendo la carne hasta que se ponga amarillenta; agregue **2** y fría-revolviendo hasta que esté aromático. Agregue **3** (Fig. 3); fría-revolviendo brevemente. Agregue **4**; haga hervir. Baje el fuego a moderado y cocine destapado por 45 minutos. Revuelva mientras se cocina hasta que parte de la salsa se haya evaporado.

3 Ponga el arroz en los dos platos a servir; ponga arriba la carne. Puede servir con vegetales.

■ Este plato es muy apetitoso debido al sabor del repollo mostaza escabechado. Debido a que este platillo tarda en cocinarse, se puede preparar y cocinar por adelantado.

Chicken & Curry Rice (Kao Mon Gai)
Pollo y Arroz al Curry

鷄腿咖哩飯

1

2

3

- Serves 2 -

1 ²/₃ lb. (750g) chicken legs

1. | ¹/₂ t. pepper
   | ¹/₂ t. curry powder

2. | ¹/₂ t. salt
   | ¹/₂ t. curry powder
   | ¹/₂ t. turmeric powder
   | 1 T. each: butter, vinegar
   | 1 ¹/₄ c. boiling water

3. | 1 c. half and half cream or milk
   | 1 ¹/₂ c. rice (do not rinse)

4. | 2 cloves of garlic, sliced
   | ¹/₄ shredded onion

5. | ¹/₄ c. each, minced: garlic,
   | onions, coriander
   | 12 cardemons (Fig. 2, optional)
   | 6 bay leaves (French
   | coriander, Fig. 3)
   | 2 T. chili soy sauce
   | 2 t. brown sugar
   | 2 c. water

   2 c. cooked rice

---

1. Remove fat from chicken legs then cut in half; sprinkle with **1**. Mix **2** well. Add **3**, stir well, cook until rice is done.

2. Heat 4 T. oil. Cook **4** over medium heat for 8 minutes until golden brown; remove and place on paper towel to absorb oil. Let cool.

3. Heat 1 T. oil. Fry chicken legs until lightly browned; add **5** and bring to boil. Reduce heat to medium; cook uncovered 50 minutes until the sauce partially evaporates (if using oven, reduce water of **5** to 1/2 c.). Partially cover, and bake at 350°F (180°C) for 50 minutes.

4. Put rice on 2 serving plates, top with chicken legs, **4** and cold pickled cucumber.

■ To make cold pickled cucumber: mix 3 T. sugar, 1/4 t. salt and 4 T. vinegar well; add 1 T. each of minced garlic, coriander, chili pepper and 1/2 c. each of shredded gherkin cucumber, and onion. Stir briefly to mix.

- 2人份 -

帶骨鷄腿3隻
　　　　……1斤4兩（750公克）

1. | 胡椒 ……………………各¹/₂小匙
   | 咖哩粉 …………………¹/₂小匙

2. | 鹽、咖哩粉 ……………各¹/₂小匙
   | 黃薑粉（圖1）…………¹/₂小匙
   | 奶油、醋 ………………各1大匙
   | 滾水 ……………………1¹/₄杯

3. | 半奶精或牛奶 …………1杯
   | 米（不洗）……………1¹/₂杯

4. | 蒜（切片）……………2瓣
   | 洋蔥（切絲）…………¹/₄個

5. | 蒜（切碎）……………¹/₄杯
   | 洋蔥（切碎）…………¹/₄杯
   | 香菜莖（切碎）………¹/₄杯
   | 卡地蒙＊（圖2，無亦可）12粒
   | 肉桂葉（法國香菜，圖3）6片
   | 辣醬油 …………………2大匙
   | 黑糖…2小匙，水　…2杯

   飯 ………………………2碗

---

1. 鷄腿切除肥肉、再切半，撒上 **1** 料。 **2** 料攪勻，再入 **3** 料拌勻煮成飯。

2. 油4大匙燒熱，入 **4** 料以中火炒約8分鐘至金黃色，置紙巾上吸油，待冷備用。

3. 油1大匙燒熱，將鷄腿煎至淡黃色，隨入 **5** 料燒開，改中火不蓋鍋煮約50分鐘至汁略收乾（若用烤箱， **5** 料內的水改爲¹/₂杯，加蓋略開小縫以350℉（180℃）烤50分鐘即可。

4. 盤內置飯，將煮好的鷄腿及炒好的 **4** 料置上，與涼拌黃瓜配食。

＊ 卡地蒙是一種香料，若無免用。

■ 涼拌黃瓜：將糖3大匙、鹽¹/₄小匙、醋4大匙先攪拌，再加切碎的蒜、香菜莖、紅辣椒各1大匙及小黃瓜片、洋蔥絲各¹/₂杯，略拌即成。

- 2 porciones -

1²/₃ lb. (750g) piernas de pollo

1. | ¹/₂ c. pimienta
   | ¹/₂ c. polvo curry

2. | ¹/₂ c. c/u: sal, polvo curry
   | ¹/₂ c. polvo de cúrcuma
   | 1 C. c/u: mantequilla, vinagre
   | 1¹/₂ tz. agua hirviendo

3. | 1 tz. crema de leche
   | 1¹/₂ tz. arroz (sin enjuagar)

4. | 2 dientes de ajo, rebanados
   | ¹/₄ cebolla picada

5. | ¹/₄ tz. c/u: ajo, cebolla,
   | cilantro, finamente picado
   | 12 cardamomos
   | (Fig. 2, opcional)
   | 6 hojas de laurel (cilantro
   | francés, Fig. 3)
   | 2 C. salsa de soya picante
   | 2 c. azúcar morena, 2 tz. agua

   2 tz. arroz cocido

---

1. Quite la grasa de las piernas de pollo, luego corte por la mitad; espolvoree con **1**. Revuelva bien **2**. Agregue **3**, revuelva bien, cocine hasta que el arroz esté listo.

2. Caliente 4 C. de aceite. Cocine **4** a fuego moderado por 8 minutos hasta que se dore; retire y ponga en toalla de papel para que se absorba el aceite. Deje enfriar.

3. Caliente 1 C. de aceite. Fría las piernas de pollo hasta que se doren ligeramente; agregue **5** y haga hervir. Baje el fuego a moderado; cocine destapado por 50 minutos hasta que la salsa se haya evaporado parcialmente (si usa horno, reduzca el agua de **5** a 1/2 tz.). Tape parcialmente y hornee a 350°F (180°C) por 50 minutos.

4. Ponga el arroz en dos platos a servir, acomode encima las piernas de pollo, **4** y el pepino escabechado frío.

■ Para preparar el pepino escabechado frío: Mezcle bien 3 C. azúcar, 1/4 c. sal y 4 C. vinagre; agregue 1 C. c/u: ajo, cilantro y chile, finamente picado y 1/2 tz. c/u: pepinos en escabeche gherkin y cebolla en rebanadas. Revuelva brevemente para que se mezcle.

Thai Sukiyaki
Sukiyaki Thai

泰式火鍋

1

2

3

- Serves 2 -	- 2人份 -	- 2 porciones -

1
- 1 T. sesame oil
- 4 c. stock or water

2 eggs

2
- Total of ½ lb. (225g), sliced: chicken, beef
- Total of ⅓ lb. (150g): shrimp, fish fillet, squid, fresh scallops

3
- ⅔ lb. (300g) nappa cabbage or other vegetables (cut in pieces)
- 1 c. sliced mushrooms
- 1 c. shredded onion

4
- 2 pieces tofu (½ lb., 225g) cut in small pieces
- 1 pkg. bean threads, softened in water

5
- 1 t. salt
- ½ c. each: sugar, vinegar, water

6
- 1 T. each (minced): garlic, coriander
- 1 T. chili paste (Fig. 1)
- ¼ c. oyster sauce
- ¼ c. fried sesame seeds (Fig. 2)
- 1 t. preserved bean curd, (Fig. 3, optional)

1
- 麻油 ·····················1大匙
- 高湯或水 ···············4杯

鷄蛋 ·····················2個

2
- 鷄、牛肉（切片） ·········共6兩（225公克）
- 蝦、魚、魷魚、鮮干貝 ·········共4兩（150公克）

3
- 大白菜或其他靑菜（切塊） ·········共半斤（300公克）
- 洋菇（切片）·············1杯
- 洋蔥（切絲）·············1杯

4
- 豆腐（切小塊）2塊 ·········6兩（225公克）
- 冬粉（泡軟）·············1小包

5
- 鹽 ·····················1小匙
- 糖 ·····················½杯
- 醋 ·····················½杯
- 水 ·····················½杯

6
- 蒜、香菜莖（切碎） 各1大匙
- 辣椒醬（圖1）···········1大匙
- 蠔油 ·····················¼杯
- 炒芝麻（圖2）···········¼杯
- 豆腐乳（圖3，無亦可）1小匙

1
- 1 C. aceite de sésamo
- 4 tz. caldo o agua

2 huevos

2
- ½ lb. (225g) en total, en rebanadas: res, pollo
- ⅓ lb (150g) en total: camarones, filete de pescado, calamar, escalope fresco

3
- ⅔ lb. (300g) repollo napa u otro vegetal (cortado en pedazos)
- 1 tz. hongos rebanados
- 1 tz. cebolla picada

4
- 2 pedazos de tofu (½ lb., 225g) cortado en pedacitos
- 1 paquete hebras de frijol, ablandados en agua

5
- 1 c. sal
- ½ tz. c/u: azúcar, vinagre, agua

6
- 1 C. c/u finamente picado: ajo, cilantro
- 1 C. pasta de chile (Fig. 1)
- ¼ tz. salsa de ostra
- ¼ tz. semillas de sésamo fritas (Fig. 2)
- 1 c. tofu preservado (Fig. 3, opcional)

---

1 Cook 5 until thick and sauce is reduced to 1/2 c. Let cool then add 6 to make dipping sauce. Divide and put in 2 bowls.

2 Bring 1 to boil in a pot and place on a butane burner. Add eggs, 2 , 3 , and 4 as desired. Dip the cooked food in dipping sauce and serve with rice. Continue to cook while serving and eating.

■ This is a cook-at-the-table dish. Place all the prepared ingredients on the table first, then enjoy eating and cooking simultaneously.

■ One of the most enjoyable aspects of eating Thai sukiyaki is the flavor from the chili dipping sauce.

---

1 將 5 料煮至½杯呈薄糊狀，待冷拌入 6 料即成沾料。分盛2碗

2 火鍋置餐桌上，將 1 料燒開，隨喜好放入準備好的蛋、 2 、 3 及 4 料，邊煮邊加，並沾沾料與飯配食。

■ 材料若準備好，即可享受邊煮邊食的樂趣。

■ 食時沾具有甜辣口味的沾料，是吃泰式火鍋的一大享受。

---

1 Cocine 5 hasta que la salsa esté espesa y reducida a 1/2 tz. Deje enfriar, luego agregue 6 para hacer una salsa para untar. Divida y póngala en 2 tazones.

2 Haga hervir 1 en una olla y ponga en una cocinilla a gas. Agregue los huevos, 2 , 3 y 4 según su gusto. Unte lo cocinado en la salsa para untar y sirva con arroz. Siga cocinando mientras continúa sirviendo y comiendo.

■ Este es un platillo para cocinar en la mesa. Ponga primero en la mesa todos los ingredientes ya preparados, luego disfrute comiendo y cocinando simultáneamente.

■ El aspecto más agradable del comer Sukiyaki Thai es el sabor de la salsa picante.